KNITTING WITH MOHAIR

KNITTING WITH MOHAIR

MELINDA COSS AND DEBBY ROBINSON

St. Martin's Press
New York

ISBN 0-312-01279-9 (pbk.)
ISBN 0-312-02029-5

First U.S. Edition
Typeset by P&M Typesetting Ltd, Exeter, U.K.
Printed in Italy by New Interlitho
10 9 8 7 6 5 4 3 2 1
Produced by the Justin Knowles Publishing Group,
9 Colleton Crescent, Exeter EX2 4BY, U.K.

CONTENTS

INTRODUCTION

Contrary to popular belief, there is no such animal as a mohair. The yarn that we know as mohair comes from the angora goat that, in turn, was named after the region in Turkey where the animal was first reared for its long luxurious coat. The term "mohair" originates from the Arabic *mukayyar*, meaning "choice or select". The name could not be more appropriate since mohair has so many outstanding qualities that make it one of the most popular natural fibers in the world. Besides being a surprisingly strong and hard-wearing fiber, in its natural state mohair also possesses a unique lustrousness. This is because the individual hairs do not have the type of serrated surface that may be observed when wool is put under the microscope. They are also much larger filaments than wool, which, since they hold air, give mohair its extraordinary thermal qualities combined with lightness. The fluffiness which immediately comes to mind when considering mohair is not, in fact, the fiber's natural condition but is produced by brushing the yarn during the spinning process.

A great deal of mohair processing and spinning is carried on in the UK, using raw material largely obtained from South Africa and Texas, the two top producers in the world today. The hair is shipped in roughly graded bales which then have to be regraded, once landed, and the grades blended according to the quality of yarn required. The hair is then washed, or "scoured", and dried before the process of "carding" may proceed. This is done by passing the hair over a series of rotating drums that are covered in teeth, thus untangling it and straightening out the individual hairs. After carding, large slivers of fiber are produced ready for "combing". This removes the shorter hairs, or "noils" and leaves the hairs lying parallel within the sliver, which is now known as a "top".

The actual spinning process now begins. First, the tops must be reduced in diameter by passing them through a series of "gill" boxes. The product of this stage is called a "roving" which is then drawn and twisted to the required thickness, ready to be mixed with any other fibers that are required.

Very little pure mohair is spun, the most common mix including approximately 20-30 per cent wool and a very small synthetic percentage that is contained within the binder yarn. This binder is fed through rollers at a slower rate than the other fibers, causing them to buckle up and form loops that are then held in position by the twisting action of the binder. Now comes the all-important brushing process when, by passing the looped yarn between two drums of fine needles, the loops are broken, producing the fluffy finish that is finally recognizable as mohair knitting yarn.

If the mohair is to be "yarn dyed" it is done at this stage, in large hanks. This produces solid colors or, alternatively, space-dyed effects, when the different parts of the hank are placed into different dyes to create a multi-colored effect within the same yarn.

Mixture shades, or "marls", are dyed at the earlier tops stage so that a number of different colors may be blended by spinning different colored tops together. This is known as "slub dyeing" and invariably produces a softer, more hairy finish since the brushing is carried out after the dyeing process and not before, as with solid colors.

As with all luxury yarns, a great deal of care should be taken in both knitting and caring for the finished garment, as described on page 125.

ABBREVIATIONS

alt	alternate
beg	begin(ning)
CB	cable back (*see* Techniques, pages 14-15)
CF	cable front (*see* Techniques, pages 14-15)
cont	continue/continuing
dec	decrease/decreasing
in	inch(es)
inc	increase/increasing
k	knit
LH	left hand
MB	make bobble (*see* Techniques, page 12)
m1	make one, i.e., inc 1 st by working into the stitch below the next st to be worked on left-hand needle, then into the stitch itself
p	purl
psso	pass slipped stitch over
repeat	repeat
rev st st	reverse st st
RH	right hand
RS	right side
sl	slip
st(s)	stitch(es)
st st	stockinette stitch
tbl	through back of loop(s)
tog	together
WS	wrong side
yb	yarn back

TECHNIQUES

READING THE CHARTS

Throughout the book explanatory charts show the color designs charted out, with stitch symbols added where necessary. Each square represents one stitch across, i.e., horizontally, and one row up, i.e., vertically. The charts should be used in conjunction with the written instructions, which will tell you where and when to incorporate them. Any colors required or symbols used will be explained in the key. Always assume that you are working in stockinette stitch unless otherwise instructed.

If you are not experienced in the use of charts, remember that when you look at the flat page you are simply looking at a graphic representation of the right side of your piece of work, i.e., the smooth side of stockinette stitch. For this reason, wherever possible, the charts begin with a right side (RS) row so that you can see exactly what is going on as you knit. Knit rows are worked from right to left and purl rows from left to right.

GAUGE

Knitting is simply a series of connecting loops, the construction of which is totally under the knitter's control. Gauge is the term used to describe the actual stitch size – its width regulating the stitch gauge measurement and its depth regulating the row gauge measurement. Obtaining a specific gauge is not a magical skill denied to all those but the initiated. It is a technicality, the controlling factor being the size of needles used by the knitter.

Since all knitting instructions are drafted to size using mathematical calculations relating to one gauge and one gauge only, that gauge must be achieved before starting the work or you will have no control whatsoever over the size of the finished garment. *This is the most important rule of knitting.*

At the beginning of every pattern, a gauge measurement will be given, using a specific stitch and needle size – e.g., "using size 8 needles and measured over st st, 18 sts and 24 rows = 4in square". You must work a gauge sample using exactly the same stitch and needle size as quoted. Cast on the number of stitches plus at least two extra because edge stitches will not be counted as they do not give

an accurate measurement. When complete, lay the gauge sample or "swatch" on a flat surface and, taking great care not to squash or stretch it, measure the gauge, using ruler and pins as shown. Using a yarn that is as fluffy as mohair can make individual stitches very difficult to see, especially with the darker colors. A handy hint is to hold the swatch up to the light when the stitches may be clearly identified, place the pins either side of the required number of stitches and then lay it down for measuring.

If there are too few stitches, your gauge is too loose. Use needles that are one size smaller to work another swatch. If there are too many stitches, your gauge is too tight. Use needles that are one size larger to work another swatch.

Even if you have to change needle sizes several times, *keep working swatches until you get it right.* You save no time by skipping this stage of the work because if you do so, you risk having to undo an entire garment that has worked out to the wrong size. You may feel that a slight difference is negligible, but a

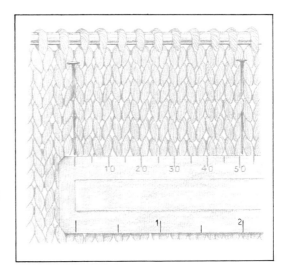

Use a ruler and pins to measure the gauge of a sample piece of knitting.

gauge measurement that is only a fraction of a stitch out per inch will result in inaccurate sizing since each fraction will have been multiplied by the number of inches across the work.

If you have had to change your needle size to achieve the correct gauge for the main stitch and if other parts of the garment are worked on different sized needles, these must also be adjusted by the same ratio. For example, if you are using needles that are one size smaller than are quoted for stockinette stitch, you must use needles that are one size smaller than are quoted for the ribbing.

We have intentionally omitted detailed reference to row gauge since many people worry over this unnecessarily, changing their needle size even though they have achieved the correct stitch gauge. Although important, row gauge does vary considerably from yarn to yarn and from knitter to knitter. If your stitch gauge is absolutely accurate, your row gauge will be only slightly out. Nevertheless, keep an eye on the work, especially when working something like a sleeve which has been calculated in rows rather than inches, and compare it with the measurement chart in case it becomes noticeably longer or shorter.

FAIRISLE

The technique of color knitting called "fairisle" is often confused with the traditional style of color knitting that originated in the Fair Isles and took its name from those islands. Knitting instructions that call for the fairisle method do not necessarily produce a small-motifed repetitive pattern, as sported by the Prince of Wales in the 1920s – far from it, as can be seen throughout this book.

The method referred to as fairisle knitting is when two colors are used across a row, with the one not in use being carried at the back of the work until it is next required. This is normally done by dropping one color and picking up the other, using the right hand. If you are lucky enough to have mastered both the "English" and "Continental" methods of knitting, each yarn may be held simultaneously, one in the left hand, the other in the right hand. The instructions below, however, are limited to the more standard one-handed method and give the three alternative methods of dealing with the yarn not in use.

Stranding
Stranding is the term used to describe the technique by which the yarn not in use is simply left hanging at the back of the work

The wrong side of weaving showing the up and down path of the carried yarn.

The wrong side of the work showing stranding at the correct gauge.

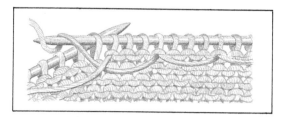

until it is next needed. The yarn in use is then dropped and the carried yarn taken up, ready for action. This means that the strand, or "float", thus produced on the wrong side of the work has a direct pull on the stitches either side of it.

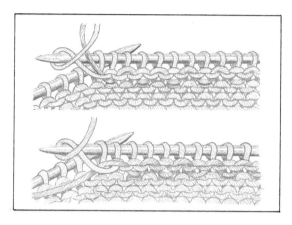

It is essential to leave a float long enough to span this gap without pulling the stitches out of shape and to allow the stitches in front of it to stretch and not to pucker on the right side of the work. It is preferable to go to the other extreme and leave a small loop at the back of the work rather than pull the float too tightly.

If the gap to be bridged by the float is wide, the strands produced may easily be caught and pulled when putting the garment on or taking it off. This may be remedied by catching the floats down with a few stitches on the wrong side of the work at the finishing stage.

Weaving
With this method the yarn being carried is looped over or under the working yarn on every stitch, creating an up and down woven effect on the wrong side of the work. Since the knitter does not have to gauge the length of the floats, many people find that this is the easiest method of ensuring an even, accurate gauge. Weaving does increase the chances of the carried color showing through on to the right side of the work, however, and it tends to produce a far more dense fabric, which is not always desirable when a thick, warm fiber such as mohair is being used.

Stranding and weaving
Combining the two methods of stranding and weaving is invariably the most practical solution to the problem of working perfect fairisle. Most designs will have color areas that will vary in the number of stitches. If the gap between areas of the same color is only a few

stitches then stranding will suffice, but if the float produced will be too long, weave in the carried yarn every few stitches. Should you be unsure about the length of float to leave, slip a finger under one. If you succeed with ease, the float is too long.

The most difficult aspect of fairisle knitting is

to get the gauge correct. This does not depend on the stitch size so much as on the way you treat the carried yarn. This is why, when working an all-over fairisle, you should always knit a gauge sample in fairisle, not in base color stockinette stitch, as the weaving or stranding will greatly affect the finished measurement of the stitches. The most important rule to remember is that *the yarn being carried must be woven or stranded loosely enough to have the same degree of "give" as the knitting itself.* Unless this is achieved, the resulting fabric will have no elasticity whatsoever, and in extreme examples very tight floats will buckle the stitches so that they lie badly on the right side of the work.

If you are working a color motif using the Fairisle technique on a single-color background, keep the gauge of the motif as close as possible to the background gauge. If there is a great difference, the motif stitches will distort the overall image.

INTARSIA

Intarsia is the term used for the technique of color knitting whereby each area of color is worked using a separate ball of yarn, rather than carrying yarns from one area to another as in the fairisle technique. Any design that involves large blocks of isolated color that are not going to be repeated along a row or required again a few rows later, should be worked in this way.

There are no limitations to the number of colors that may be used on any one row, other than those imposed by lack of patience and/or dexterity. Avoid getting into a tangle with too many separate balls of yarn hanging from the back of the work, and remember that every time a new ball of yarn is introduced and broken off after use, two extra ends are produced that will have to be secured at the end of the day. When ends are left, always make sure that they are long enough to thread

up so that they may be properly fastened with a pointed tapestry needle. Do this very carefully through the backs of the worked stitches so as not to distort the design on the right side of the work. The ends that are left should never be knotted because they will make the wrong side of the work look extremely unsightly as well as invariably working themselves loose and creating problems at a later stage.

If only a few large, regular areas of color are being worked, then, to avoid any tangling of the wool, lay the different balls of yarn on a table in front of you or keep them separate in individual jam jars or shoe-boxes. However, this requires careful turning at the end of every row so that the various strands do not become twisted.

The easiest method of all is to use small bobbins that hold each yarn separately, hanging at the back of the work. These are available at most large yarn stores or may be made at home out of stiff card. They come in a variety of shapes, but all have a narrow slit in them that keeps the wound yarn in place but allows the knitter to unwind a controlled amount as and when required. When winding yarn on to a bobbin, try to wind sufficient to complete an entire area of color, but don't

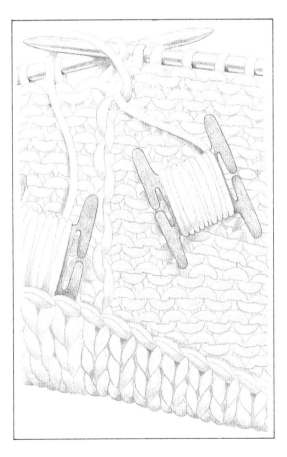

Stranding and weaving worked too tightly.

If you are using the intarsia method, twist the yarns firmly together when you change colors.

11

overwind as heavy bobbins may pull stitches out of shape.

When actually changing color from one stitch to another, it is vital that you twist the yarns around one another before dropping the old color and working the first stitch in the new color as shown. This prevents a hole from forming. If it is not done, there is no strand to connect the last stitch worked in color "A" to the first stitch worked in color "B". This twisting should also be done quite firmly to prevent a gap from appearing after the work has settled.

The four steps in making a bobble are illustrated here. Remember, if you work a bobble on the wrong side, push it through to the right side of your work.

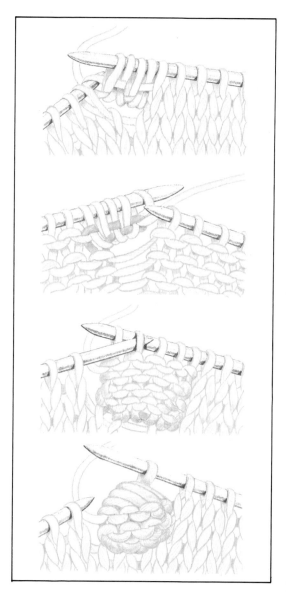

If you use beads with a fairly large hole, it is possible to knit them into the work and so avoid having to thread each bead on to the yarn before knitting.

MAKING A BOBBLE

There are numerous variations on the theme of bobble making but, for simplicity, wherever the "MB" abbreviation occurs in this book, it refers to a basic five-stitch bobble with four

rows being worked over the bobble stitches only. If worked on a right side (RS) row, the bobble will hang on the right side; if worked on a wrong side (WS) row, push it through on to the right side.

1. When the MB position on the row has been reached, make five stitches out of the next one by knitting into its front, then its back, front, back and front again, before slipping it off the left-hand needle.
2. Turn the work and knit these five stitches only.
3. Turn the work, p5. Repeat the last two rows.
4. Using the point of the left-hand needle, lift bobble stitches, in order, over the first one on the right-hand needle, i.e., 2nd, 3rd and 4th, 5th, so that one stitch remains.

After completing the bobble, the work may continue as normal, the single stitch having been restored to its original position on the row.

BEADING

When using beads that have a fairly large hole, there is a method of knitting them into the work that avoids the usual laborious process of having to thread every bead on to the yarn before knitting.

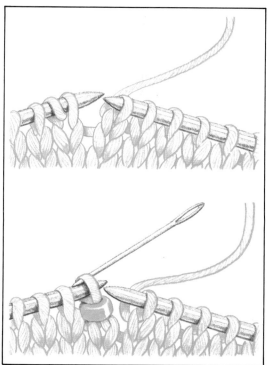

1. The stitch immediately below the one that is to receive the bead is worked normally, but instead of putting the yarn around the needle once, it is done twice. (**NOTE:** This should not be confused with "yarn over needle" before knitting a stitch, which is a method of creating a new stitch. By putting the needle into the stitch and then putting the yarn around the needle twice before working it, you are simply producing an elongated stitch when it is worked on the next row.)

2. On the next row, when the bead position is reached, the two strands are slipped off the left-hand needle, thus forming the elongated stitch that may then be passed through the bead with the aid of a very small crochet hook or a tapestry needle.

3. The stitch is then placed back on to the left-hand needle and is worked normally.

The bead should sit vertically, with the stitch running straight through it so that it is visible on both sides of the work.

CROCHET CHAIN

A crochet chain is so basic that it requires no prior knowledge of crochet. Simple and speedy to work, care should still be taken to keep the size of the chain loops as uniform as possible and not to twist the chain as you work, i.e., it should be held in exactly the same position throughout. It is worked as follows:

1. Form a slip loop with your fingers (leaving a non-working end long

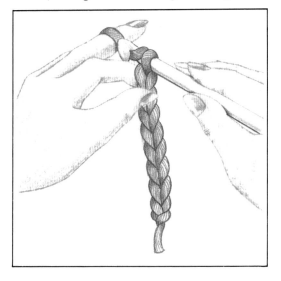

enough to attach the chain eventually to the knitting).

2. Place the crochet hook through the loop and around the yarn as shown.

3. Pull the loop through.

Keep repeating stages 2 and 3 until the chain is the required length. Pull the yarn end through the final loop to secure.

TURNING

Turning is also called "working short rows" since this is precisely what is being done. By turning the work in mid-row and leaving part of it unworked, shaping is created since one side of the work will have more rows than the other. If the work is then bound off, a sloping edge will result, making it ideal for shoulder shaping instead of the more usual method of binding off groups of stitches to produce noticeable "steps".

Turning is not advisable when you are working complicated stitches or color patterns, as working short rows will invariably throw them out.

Unfortunately, even when care is taken,

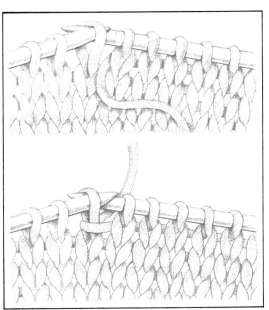

The first stages of turning to ensure that holes do not form.

there is a tendency for holes to form at the points where the work is turned. There is a method whereby these holes may be completely eliminated. Although this looks complicated at first, the finished effect is well worth the effort involved in mastering the technique.

This method may be used on right or wrong side rows. Here it has been illustrated on the right side of stockinette stitch.

Make sure that all the loops are of a uniform length when you work a crochet chain.

The front cross cable.

1. Knit to the point where turning is indicated, but before doing so bring the yarn to the front of the work and slip the next stitch from the left-hand to the right-hand needle.
2. Put the yarn to the back of the work and return the slipped stitch to the left-hand needle.
3. Now turn work, purl to end.

Repeat the last three steps at every turning point.

Since all the stitches must now be worked across, if the turned shaping is being worked immediately before binding off or knitting a seam, you should add an extra row. Work to

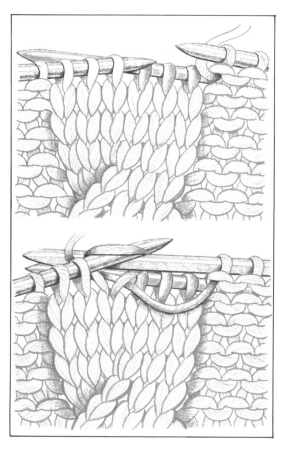

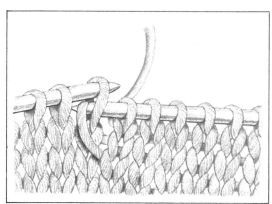

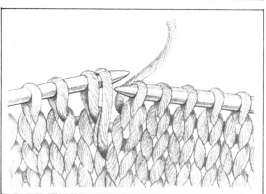

The final steps of turning.

the first stitch which has had a loop made around it by putting the yarn forward and then back.

1. First, slip this stitch from the left-hand needle to the right-hand needle, lifting the strand of the loop up on to the right-hand needle together with the stitch.
2. Slip both strand and stitch back to the left-hand needle, straightening them as you do so.
3. Knit the stitch and strand together.

Work to the next "looped" stitch and repeat the process.

When this row is completed, the work may be continued as normal.

CABLES

A basic cable is simply a twist in the knitted fabric caused by working a small number of stitches out of sequence every few rows. This is done by slipping the stitches on to a needle and leaving them at the front or the back of the work while the next stitches on the left-hand needle are worked. The held stitches are then worked normally.

The cable, worked in stockinette stitch, will invariably be flanked by a few reversed stockinette stitches in order to give it definition. Since it does involve a twist, however, a cabled fabric will always have a tighter gauge than one worked in plain stockinette stitch, so take extra care when working a gauge sample.

Cable needles are very short and double-pointed. Some have a little kink in them to help keep the stitches in place while others are being worked. Use one that is a similar size to the needles being used for the main work and take care not to stretch or twist the stitches when you are moving them from needle to needle.

On the right side of the work, if the stitches

are held to the front, the cable will cross from the right to the left. If the stitches are held at the back of the work, the cable will twist from the left to the right.

Front cross cable
1. (RS): Work to the six stitches that are to be cabled. Slip the next three stitches on the left-hand needle on to the cable needle and leave them hanging at the front of the work.
2. Knit the next three stitches on the left-hand needle as normal.
3. Knit the three held stitches off the cable needle.

Repeat this twist wherever indicated in the instructions.

The same basic technique may be used to move a single stitch across a background of stockinette stitch at a diagonal, rather than form a cable that moves up the work vertically. This is used in the Beaded Sweater pattern on page 25.

Where the abbreviation CB2 is used, the first stitch is slipped onto the cable needle and left at the back of the work while the next stitch is knitted. The held stitch is then knitted off the cable needle. CF2 is the same but with the cable needle left at the front of the work. On the purl rows the abbreviation pCB2 and pCF2 are used to denote the same movement but where the stitches are purled rather than knitted. In this way a continuous criss-cross line is formed.

SEAMS
After achieving the correct gauge, the final sewing up of your knitting is the most important technique to master. It can make or break a garment, however carefully it may have been knitted. This is why the finishing instructions after every set of knitting instructions should be followed to the letter, with particular reference to the type of seam and the order in which the seams are to be worked.

Before starting any piece of work, always leave an end of yarn long enough to complete a substantial section of the eventual seam, if not the whole thing. After working a couple of rows, wind this up and pin it to the work to keep it out of the way. If required, also leave a sizable end when the work has been completed. This saves having to join in new ends that may well work loose, especially at stress points.

The secret of perfect-looking seams is uniformity and regularity of stitch. When joining two pieces that have been worked in the same stitch, they should be joined row for

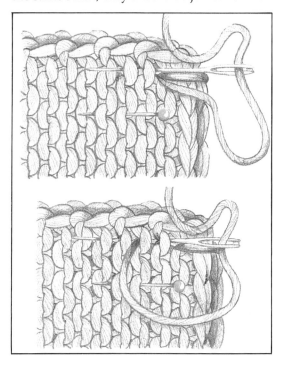

If you use backstitch to join a seam and you are starting at the very edge of the work, close the edges with an overstitch before beginning the row of backstitch.

row and all work should be pinned first to ensure an even distribution of fabrics. When joining work that has a design on both pieces, take great care to match the colors, changing the color you are using to sew the seam where necessary.

Backstitch
Pin the two pieces of work together, right sides facing, making sure that the edges are absolutely flush. Always leave as narrow a seam allowance as possible to reduce unnecessary bulk. It is essential that the line of backstitches is kept straight, using the lines of the knitted stitches as a guide. Each stitch should be identical in length, one starting immediately after the previous one has finished. On the side of the work facing you

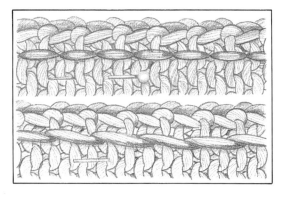

When you use backstitch to join a seam, the finished seam should be perfectly straight; the diagrams illustrate the appearance of the front (top) and back (below) of the completed seam.

this should form a continuous, straight line. If the seam is starting at the very edge of the work, close the edges with an overstitch as shown. Now work the backstitch as follows:

1. Make a running stitch (maximum length ½in), through both thicknesses of work.
2. Put the needle back into the work in exactly the same spot as before and make another running stitch twice as long.
3. Put the needle back into the work adjacent to the point where the previous stitch ended. Make another stitch the same length.

Keep repeating step 3 until the last stitch, which needs to be half as long to fill in the final gap left at the end of the seam.

By keeping the stitch line straight and by pulling the yarn fairly firmly after each stitch, no gaps should appear when the work is opened out and the seam pulled apart.

This seam is suitable for lightweight yarns or where an untidy selvedge has been worked.

Flat seam
This seam is a slight contradiction in terms since its working involves an oversewing action, but when the work is opened out it will do so completely and lie quite flat, unlike a backstitched seam.

A blunt-ended tapestry needle should be used to avoid splitting the knitted stitches. After pinning both pieces right sides together, the work should be held as shown. The needle is then placed through the very edge stitch on the back piece and then through the very edge stitch on the front piece. The yarn is pulled through and the action repeated, always placing the needle through exactly the same part of each stitch every time. Always work through the edge stitch only. By taking in more than this, a lumpy, untidy seam will be produced that will never lie flat.

When two pieces of stockinette stitch are to be joined with a flat seam, do not work any special selvedge such as knitting every edge stitch. Just work the edge stitches normally but as tightly as possible, using only the tip of your needle. When you come to work the seam, place the needle behind the knots of the edge stitches and not the looser strands that run between the knots since these will not provide a firm enough base for the seam, which will appear gappy when opened out.

Flat seams are essential for heavy-weight yarns where a backstitch would create far too much bulk. They should also be used for attaching buttonbands, collars, and so on where flatness and neatness are essential.

Borders, waistbands, cuffs and any other part of a garment where the edge of the seam

Right: the diagrams show how you should hold the knitting to work a flat seam and how the work will look on the right side.

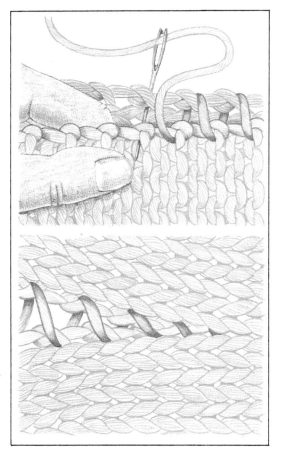

Far right: use sewn slip stitch to attach a pocket to a garment.

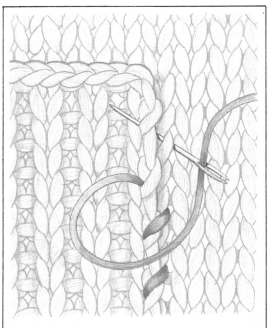

will be visible should be joined with a flat seam, even if the remainder of the garment is to have a backstitched seam. Start with a flat seam until the rib/border is complete and then change over to a backstitch, taking in a tiny seam allowance at first and then smoothly widening it without making a sudden inroad into the work.

Sewn slip stitch

Where one piece of work is to be placed on top of another, for example, when turning in a

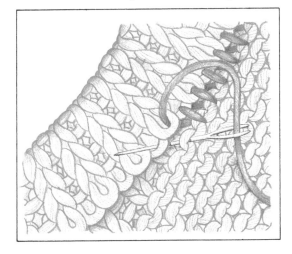

double neckband, folding over a hem or attaching the edges of pocket borders, a sewn slip stitch should be used.

When turning in a neckband that has been bound off, the needle should be placed through the bound-off edge and then through the exact same stitch but on the row where it was initially knitted up. It is essential to follow the line of the stitch in this way to avoid twisting the neckband. By repeating the action, the visible sewn stitch runs at a diagonal.

The same rule applies when sewing down a neckband that has not been bound off but which has had its stitches held on a thread. The only difference is that the needle is placed through the actual held stitch, thus securing it. When each stitch has been slip-stitched down, the thread may be removed. This method allows for a neckband with more "give" than one which has been bound off.

On pocket borders use the line of stitches on the main work as a guide to produce a perfectly straight vertical line of stitches. Place the needle through one strand of the main work stitch and then behind the knot of the border edge stitch, as for a flat seam.

KNITTED SHOULDER SEAMS

This method of joining is perfect for shoulders on which no shaping has been worked or on which the shaping has been worked by turning rows, as described on page 13. It creates an extremely neat, flat seam.

Since the two pieces to be joined must be worked stitch for stitch, they must both have exactly the same number of stitches. Even though the pattern specifies that you should have a certain number of stitches at this point, it is wise to double check the number you actually have on your needles since it is very easy to lose or gain the odd stitch accidentally along the way.

The technique itself involves the use of three needles. The stitches from the front and back are held on their respective needles, both in the left hand, while the right hand holds a third, larger, needle which helps to prevent the bound-off stitches from becoming too tight. Holding more than one needle in the hand and trying to work through two stitches at a time without dropping them can seem very awkward at first, but with a little practice it feels like normal knitting.

The needles are held with the right sides of the work facing one another and with the stitches lined up at corresponding intervals on the front and back needles.

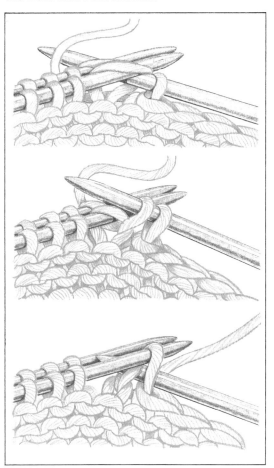

Use sewn slip stitch to hold a double neckband in position.

The diagrams illustrate the three steps involved in knitting shoulder seams together. You must always have exactly the same number of stitches on the two pieces that are to be joined in this way.

1. The point of the right-hand needle is put through the first stitch on the front needle and the first stitch on the back needle, with exactly the same action as a regular knit stitch but going through both simultaneously.
2. Pull a loop through to form a single stitch on the right-hand needle, the old stitches being slipped off the left-hand needle.
3. Steps 1 and 2 are repeated so that there are two stitches on the right-hand needle. The second stitch is then lifted over the first, as in regular binding off.

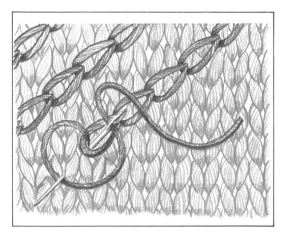

Step 3 should be repeated across all the stitches to be knitted together until one loop remains on the right-hand needle. Pull the yarn through this to secure it.

When you are knitting together a shoulder seam on a garment where no neck shaping has been worked and the neck stitches have not been bound off, all the stitches on the back may be dealt with at the same time. By starting to work the first shoulder together from the armhole to the neck edge, the back neck stitches may then be bound off (if the pattern requires that they are bound off), without breaking the yarn, which may then be used to knit together the second shoulder seam.

Normally worked on the inside of the work to create an extremely neat, flat and durable seam on the right side of the work, a knitted seam may be worked with the wrong sides of the knitting facing one another. This creates a decorative ridge on the right side of the work.

EMBROIDERY

When working figurative motifs, it is not always possible to create a detailed, accurate picture using knitting alone, since you are always ruled by the size and structure of the stitch itself. The addition of embroidery gives that much more flexibility. A small backstitch, as described on page 15 is the most useful stitch for creating a single line, but where a more ornamental effect is required, as on the Peacock Jumper (page 85), chain stitch should be used. It is worked as follows:

1. Bring the needle through to the right side of the work.
2. Place it back through the hole from which it has emerged and up in again in whichever direction the line of chain is to be worked.
3. Loop the working yarn/thread under the needle as shown.
4. Pull the needle through loosely so that the chain "link" is not closed.

Keep repeating steps 2-4.

NOTE TO READER

The mohair yarns needed for the projects in this book vary in gauge from worsted to bulky weight. Please check with your yarn dealer for the appropriate weight mohair for the individual project(s) you are working on.

AUTUMN GLORY JACKET

A square-shaped, shawl-collared jacket for
wind-blown days and autumn nights. Worked
using the intarsia method.

Materials
Yarnworks mohair – 18oz
of main color and 1oz each
of three contrasting colors,
3 × 1½in buttons.
Needles
One pair of No. 8 and one
pair of No. 9 needles.
Gauge
Using No. 9 needles and
measured over st st, 16 sts
and 20 rows × 4in square.

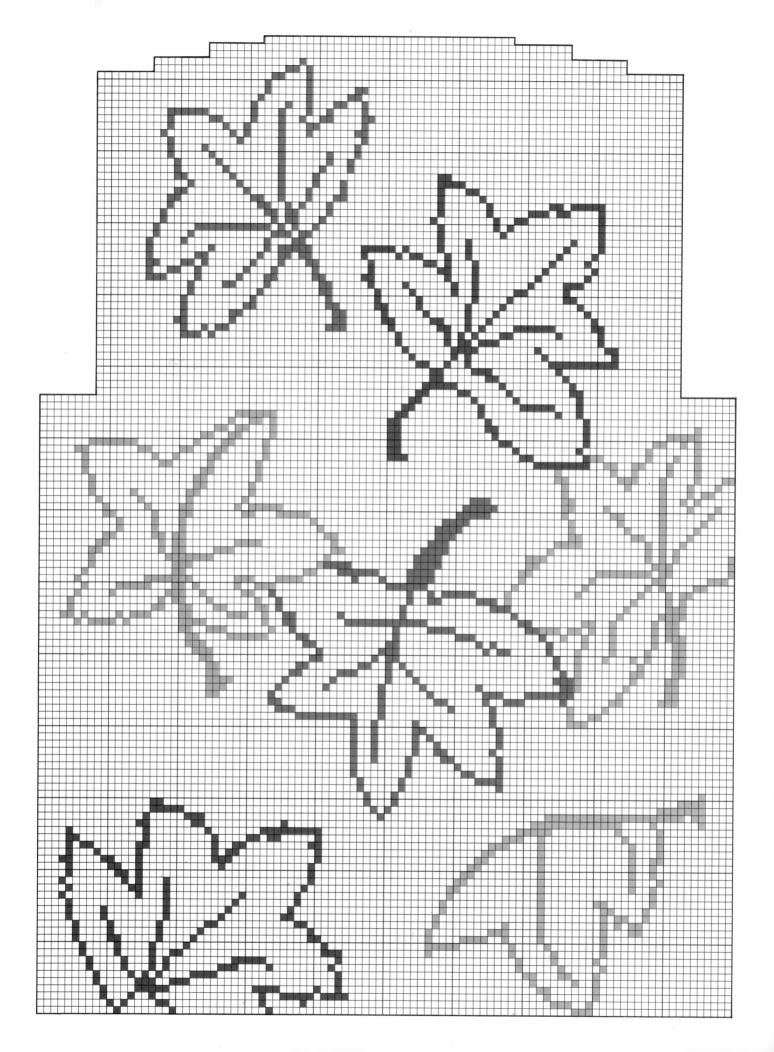

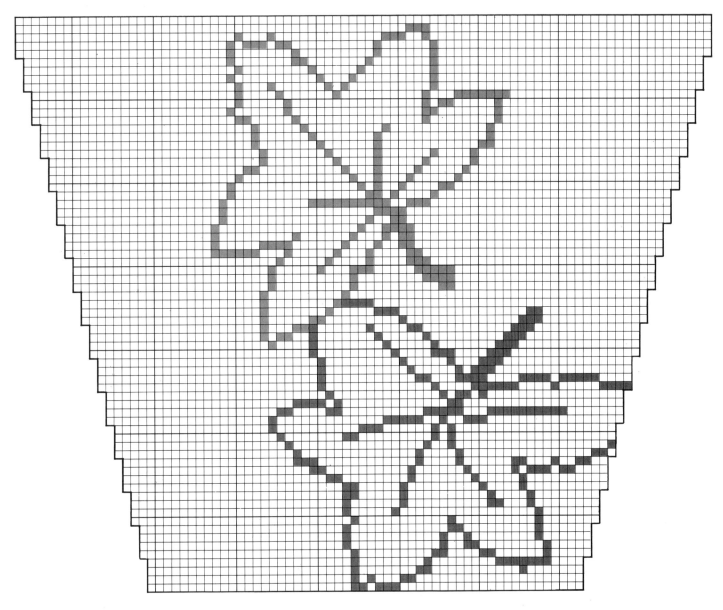

Back

Using No. 8 needles and main color, cast on 100 sts. Row 1: *k1, p1, rep from * to end. Row 2: *p1, k1, rep from * to end. Repeat these last 2 rows of moss st twice more. Change to No. 9 needles and begin following the chart in st st, starting with a knit row. Follow chart to row 85. Bind off 8 sts at the beg of the next 2 rows. Cont straight until shoulder shaping. Bind off 8 sts at beg of next 6 rows. Bind off remaining 36 sts.

Left front

Using No. 8 needles and main color, cast on 52 sts. Row 1: *k1, p1, rep from * to end. Row 2: *p1, k1, rep from * to end. Repeat these last 2 rows of moss st twice more. Change to 5 No. 9 needles and, starting with a knit row, begin following the chart in st st. Follow chart to row

86. **Shape armhole**: bind off 8 sts at beg of next row. Still following the chart, work 4 rows, then **shape neck** as follows: while working straight at armhole edge, dec 1 st at neck edge every alt row, 15 times, then work other without shaping, following chart to shoulder. Row 132: bind off 8 sts at beg of this row and the next 2 alt rows. Bind off remaining 5 sts.

Right front

Work as for left front, reversing shapings.

Sleeves

Using No. 9 needles, cast on 54 sts. K1, p1 rib for 7in. Starting with a knit row, begin following chart in st st, inc 1 st each end of every 4th row until you have 86 sts. Work 5 more rows until chart is complete. Bind off loosely.

The chart opposite (page 20) is for the back; above is the chart for the left sleeve (reverse the colors for the right sleeve); overleaf (page 22) are the charts for the left and right fronts.

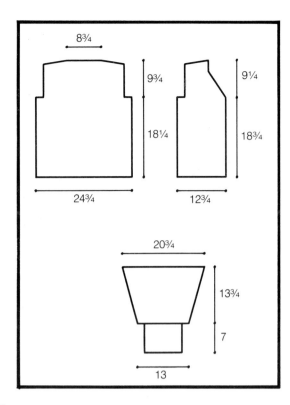

Buttonband collar

Using No. 8 needles, cast on 18 sts and work in k1, p1 rib until the band, when slightly stretched, reaches the start of the neck shaping, ending with a WS row. Next row: *rib 2 (k1, p1, k1) into next st, rib to end. Rib 3 rows. Repeat last 4 rows 14 times more (48 sts). Cont in rib without further shaping until the band reaches the center back of neck. Bind off loosely.

Buttonhole band

Repeat as for buttonband until 28 rows have been completed. Next row: rib 7 sts, bind off 4 sts, rib 7 sts. Next row: rib 7 sts, cast on 4 sts, rib 7 sts. Complete as for buttonband, making buttonholes as described above on rows 53 and 78.

Finishing

Sew all seams with a flat seam. Stitch the collar and buttonhole band into place. Attach buttons.

BEADED SWEATER

A delicate drop-shoulder, wide V-neck sweater, the lattice pattern being highlighted with golden beads. These are attached individually and do not have to be threaded on to the yarn at the beginning of the work (*see* Techniques, page 12).

Materials
Yarnworks mohair – 18oz.
189 beads with large holes.
Needles
One pair of No. 6 and one pair of No. 8 needles.
Gauge
Using No. 8 needles and measured over pattern, 18 sts and 24 rows = 4in square.

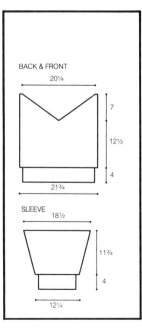

BACK & FRONT
20¼
7
12½
4
21¾

SLEEVE
18½
11¾
4
12¼

Pattern

Row 1 (RS): k1,* CF2, k9, CB2, k1, CF2, k9, CB2, k1. Rep from * to end.

Row 2: *p2, pCB2, p7, pCF2, p3, pCB2, p7, pCF2, p1. Rep from * to last st, p1.

Row 3: k1, *k2, CF2, k5, CB2, k5, CF2, k5, CB2, k3. Rep from * to end.

Row 4: *p4, pCB2, p3, pCF2, p7, pCB2, p3, pCF2, p3. Rep from * to last st, p1.

Row 5: k1, *k4, CF2, yarn twice, k1, CB2, k9, CF2, yarn twice, k1, CB2, k5. Rep from * to end.

Row 6: purl, placing a bead on to every "yarn" stitch from previous row (*see* Techniques, page 12).

Row 7: k1, * k4, CB2, k1, CF2, k9, CB2, k1, CF2, k5. Rep from * to end.

Row 8: * p4, pCF2, p3, pCB2, p7, pCF2, p3, pCB2, p3. Rep from * to last st, p1.

Row 9: k1, * k2, CB2, k5, CF2, k5, CB2, k5, CF2, k3. Rep from * to end.

Row 10: * p2, pCF2, p7, pCB2, p3, pCF2, p7, pCB2, p1. Rep from * to last st, p1.

Row 11: k1, * CB2, k9, CF2, yarn twice, k1, CB2, k9, CF2, yarn twice, k1. Rep from * to end, but working the final st of the row as a normal knit st.

Row 12: row 6.

Repeat these 12 rows for pattern.

Front and back

(Both worked identically.)

Using No. 6 needles, cast on 90 sts.

Row 1: * k1, p1, rep from * to end. Keep repeating this row to form a single rib for 4in, ending with an RS row. Purl the next row, inc into every 10th st (99 sts). Now change to No. 8 needles and cont in pattern (3 ½ repeats of the pattern fit into the row), omitting any "yarn twice" or bead sts where they come too close to the edge of the work.

Work straight for 6 ½ patterns, ending with a bead row. **Divide for neck**: work 49 sts, bind off the central st and work pattern to end. Cont with this set of sts only, leaving the others on a holder.

Keeping in pattern, but omitting the yarn and bead where they fall near the neck edge, dec 1 st at neck edge on every row except on bead rows where a double dec is worked as follows: work pattern to last 3 sts, p2 tog and place this st back on to LH needle, slip last st over this and return it to the RH needle. When 3 sts remain, bind off. Return to other side of neck and shape to match, working the double decs as p3 tog. When 3 sts remain, bind off.

Sleeves

Using No. 6 needles, cast on 38 sts and work in single rib for 4in, ending on an RS row. Purl the next row, inc into every other st (57 sts). Now change to No. 8 needles and cont in pattern (2 repeats will fit across the row to start with). Inc 1 st each end of every 5th row, keeping these new sts in pattern as you go. By the time 6 pattern repeats have been worked the length of the sleeve, 85 sts should be on the needle. Bind off loosely.

Neckband

Join the 3 sts either side of each shoulder with a flat seam. Using No. 6 needles and with RS of work facing, knit up 56 sts along the RS of neck from the very point of the front "V" to the shoulder seam. Knit up 1 st from the shoulder seam (this to become the axial st), then knit up 56 sts down the back to the point of the "V". Work in single rib, dec 1 st either side of the axial st (which is always knitted on a RS row and purled on a WS row), on every alt row. When the rib is 2¾in in depth, bind off in rib. Work the same on the left side of the neck.

Finishing

Open out the body and pin the sleeves into position, taking care not to bunch them. Join with a flat seam. Join the side and sleeve seams similarly. Cross over the neckband at the "V" points and carefully slip st down along the knit up lines.

BAT-WING LEAVES AND BOBBLES JUMPER

A sophisticated, one-size bat-wing jumper suitable for evening or day wear. Worked in stockinette stitch using the intarsia method and enhanced with bobbles.

Materials
Yarnworks mohair – 11oz main color ("A"); 3oz of lemon and peach ("B" and "D"); and 3½oz of mint ("C").
NOTE: Where an "X" is shown on the chart, make a bobble in peach; where a circle is shown, make a bobble in lemon (*see* Techniques, page 12).
Needles
One pair of No. 7 and one pair of No. 9 needles.
Gauge
Using No. 9 needles and measured over st st, 16 sts and 20 rows = 4in square.

The chart opposite (page 29) should be incorporated into both the front and the back.

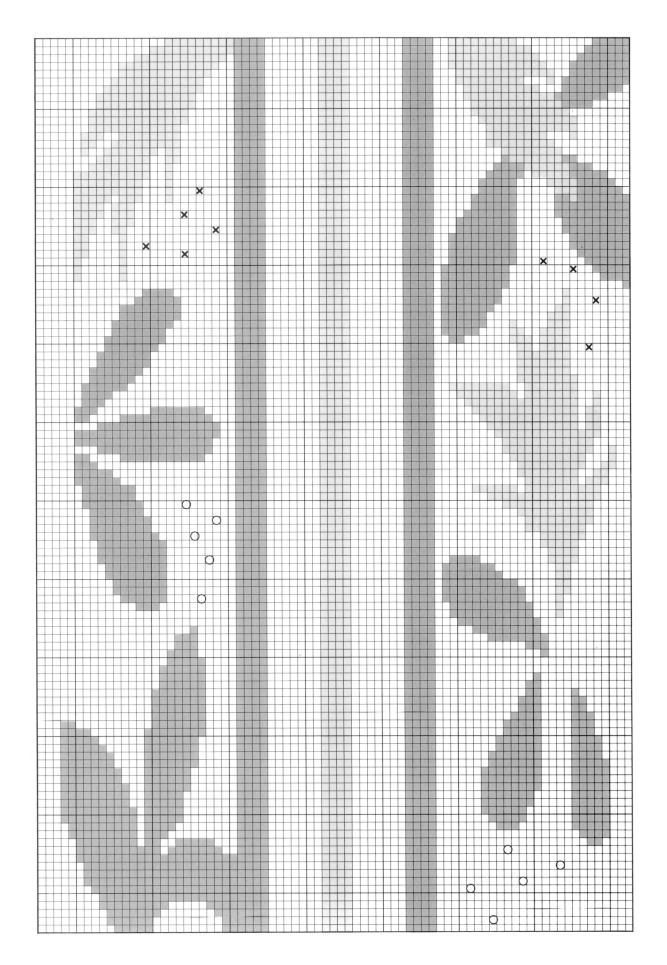

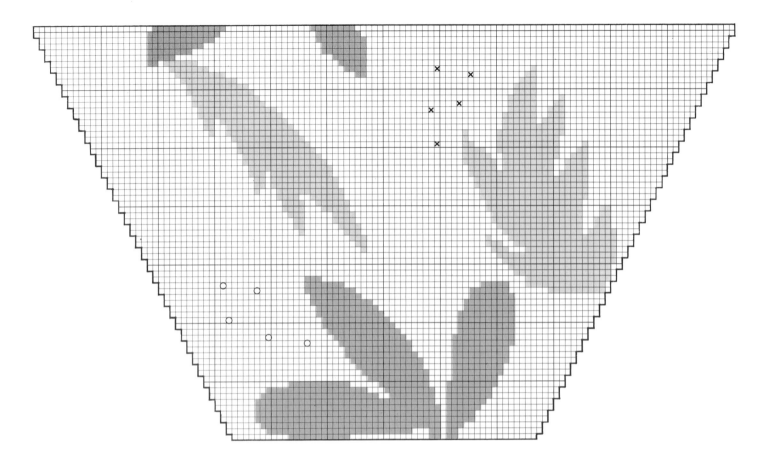

Incorporate the chart above into both left and right sleeves.

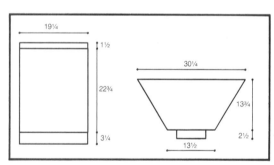

Front and back

Using No. 7 needles, cast on 78 sts in color "C". Work 4 rows in k1, p1 rib. Change to color "A" and work 12 rows in k1, p1 rib. Change to No. 9 needles and, beginning with a knit row, begin following chart in st st, placing bobbles, where indicated, in the colors stated. When the chart has been worked, change to No. 7 needles and color "A" and work 8 rows in k1, p1 rib. Bind off loosely in ribbing.

Left sleeve

Using No. 7 needles and color "C", cast on 32 sts. Work 4 rows in k1, p1 rib. Change to color "A" and work 8 more rows in k1, p1 rib. Using main color, work next row as follows: rib 5, inc 22 sts by knitting twice into each of the next 22 sts, rib to end (54 sts). Change to No. 9 needles and, beginning with a knit row, follow chart in st st (except where bobbles are indicated), inc 1 st each end of the next row and every alt row until chart is complete and 71 rows have been worked (124 sts). Bind off loosely.

Right sleeve

Work as for left sleeve, leaving out the top two motifs shown on the sleeve chart which use color "B".

Finishing

Sew in all loose ends securely. The seams throughout are flat seams. Lay out the front and back, RS tog, and pin them tog 4¾in in from each top rib edge to make shoulder seams. Join sleeve and body seams, taking care to match the patterns where the left sleeve joins the body. **NOTE:** The center sleeve top should be joined to the top of the neck rib where the shoulder seam finishes.

CARMEN MIRANDA SWEATER

Dance away the night in this colorful crew-
necked, stockinette stitch, picture sweater.
Worked using the intarsia method.

Materials
Yarnworks mohair – 7oz
emerald, 3oz each of red
and turquoise, 1¾oz
brown, yellow and black;
less than 1oz of orange,
gold, fuchsia, purple,
mauve, peach, white.
NOTE: Where an "X" is
shown on the chart, make a
bobble in the appropriate
color (*see* Techniques, page
12).
Needles
One pair of No. 7 and one
pair of No. 10 needles.
Gauge
Using No. 10 needles and
measured over st st, 16 sts
and 18 rows = 4in square.

The chart opposite (page 33)
should be incorporated into
the front of the sweater.

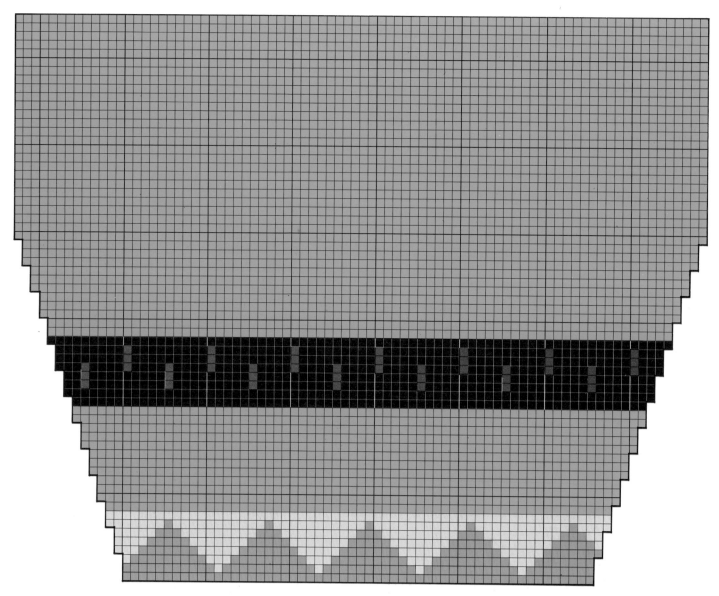

The chart above should be incorporated into the right sleeve.

Front

Using No. 7 needles and turquoise, cast on 70 st. K1, p1 rib for 3½in, ending with a WS row. Next row: *rib 4, inc in next st. Repeat from * 13 more times (84 sts). Change to No. 10 needles and begin following the chart in st st, starting with a knit row.** Work straight until 99 rows have been completed. **Shape neck**: row 100: p28 sts. Leave these sts on a spare needle, bind off 28 sts. P28 sts. Working on this last set of 28 sts, dec 1 st at neck edge on the next 4 rows. Next row: still dec 1 st at neck edge, bind off 9 sts at beg of row for the shoulder. Work 1 row, bind off remaining 13 sts. Repeat for other side of neck, reversing shapings.

Back

Work as for front to **. Begin following chart (page 36) for back in st st until 34 rows have been completed. Change to emerald and work straight in st st until back matches front to shoulder shaping. Bind off 9 sts at beg of next 2 rows, then bind off remaining 66 sts.

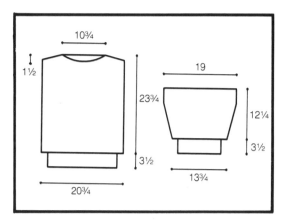

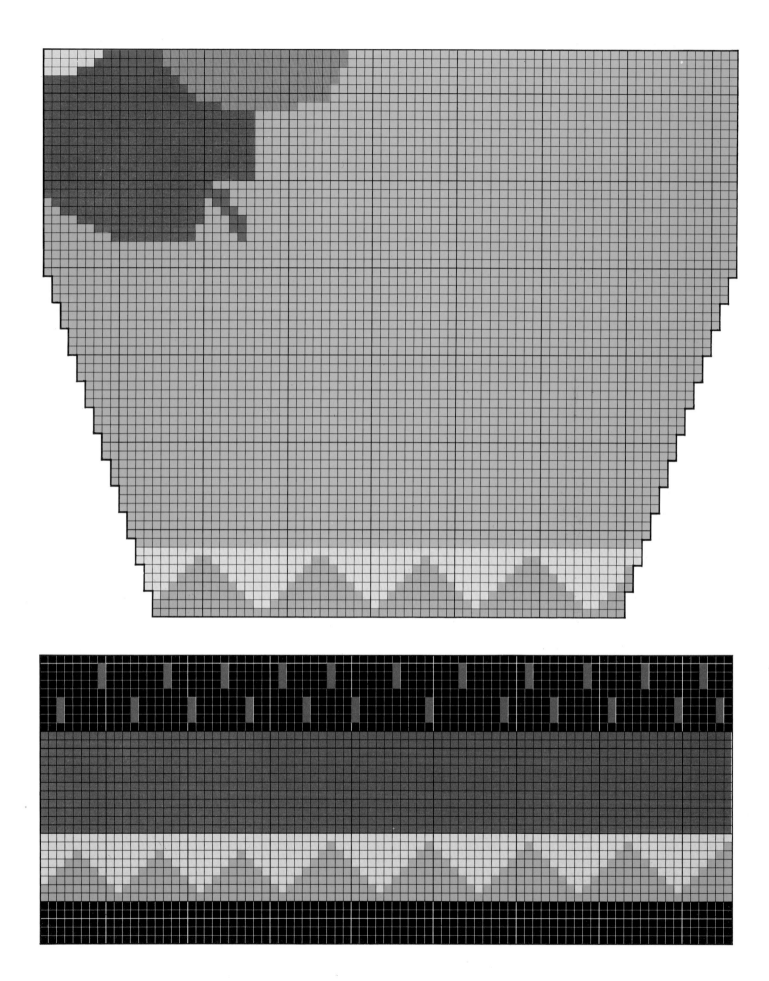

Right sleeve

Using No. 7 needles and black, cast on 36 sts. K1, p1 rib for 3½in, inc 20 sts evenly along last row of rib. Change to No. 10 needles and cont following sleeve chart (page 34) in st st, inc 1 st each end of every 3rd row until you have 82 sts. Work straight without shaping for 25 more rows. Bind off loosely.

Left sleeve

Work as for right sleeve, but following left sleeve chart (page 36). Backstitch left shoulder seams.

Neckband

With RS of work facing, No. 7 needles and emerald, pick up 7 sts down right front side, 28 sts center front, 7 sts up left front side and 40 sts from center back (86 sts). K1, p1 rib for 9 rows. Bind off loosely in ribbing. Turn neckband inwards and slip stitch bound-off edge to "pick up" edge.

Finishing

Backstitch remaining shoulder seam, then, using flat seams, join sleeves to body, taking care to match the fruit on top left sleeve to front. Join side and sleeve seams.

The chart opposite above should be incorporated into the left sleeve; the chart opposite below should be incorporated into the back.

CHECKERS SWEATER

A shawl-neck, drop-shoulder sweater in a striking checker-board pattern using the fairisle method of color knitting (*see* Techniques, page 10). The instructions are for women's/men's sizes throughout.

Materials
Yarnworks mohair – grey (G): 11/12oz; natural (N): 7/9oz; black (B): 7/9oz.
Needles
One pair of No. 7 and one pair of No. 9 needles.
Gauge
Using No. 9 needles and measured over pattern, 16 sts and 23 rows = 4in square.

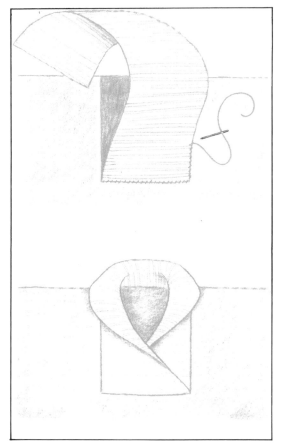

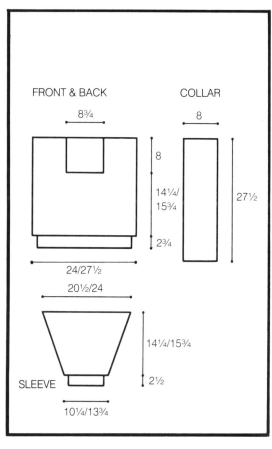

FRONT & BACK	COLLAR

FRONT & BACK: 8¾, 8, 14¼/15¾, 2¾, 24/27½

COLLAR: 8, 27½

SLEEVE: 20½/24, 14¼/15¾, 2½, 10¼/13¾

Pattern

Row 1: * K7 black, (p1 natural, yb, k1 black), 3 times, p1 natural, yb, rep from * to end.

Row 2: * (p1 black, k1 natural, yb), 3 times, p8 black, rep from * to end.

Repeat these 2 rows, 3 times more.

Row 9: * (p1 grey, yb, k1 black), 3 times, p1, k7, grey, rep from * to end.

Row 10: * p7 grey (p1 black, k1 grey, yb), 3 times, p1 black, rep from * to end.

Repeat these 2 rows three times more.

Row 17: * k7 natural (p1 grey, yb, k1 natural), 3 times, p1 grey, yb, rep from * to end.

Row 18: * (p1 natural, k1 grey, yb), 3 times, p8 natural, rep from * to end.

Repeat these 2 rows 3 times more.

Now repeat these 24 rows but alternating the color order so that row 25 will start p1 natural, yb, k1 black.

These 48 rows form the pattern and are repeated throughout.

Back

Using No. 7 needles and grey, cast on 84/98 sts. Row 1: * k1, p1, rep from * to end. Keep repeating this row to form single rib for 2¾in. Rib the next row, inc every 6th/7th st (98/112 sts). Now change to No. 9 needles and cont in pattern until 14/15 individual squares have been worked. Bind off.

Front

As for back until 9/10 individual squares have been worked. **Divide for neck**: work pattern for 31/38 sts, bind off 36 sts, work pattern to end. Cont with this set of sts, leaving others on a holder. Work until the front matches the back. Bind off. Return to held sts, joining yarn in at neck edge. Work to match first side of neck.

Sleeves

Using No. 7 needles and grey, cast on 36/42 sts and work in single rib for 2½in. Rib the next row, inc into every 6th/3rd st, (42/56 sts). Now change to No. 9 needles and cont in pattern, inc 1 st each end of every 4th row, keeping all new sts in pattern as you go.

When you have 70/90 sts, start inc 1 st each end of every alt row until you have 84/98 sts. Work straight until 9/10 individual squares have been completed. Bind off loosely.

Collar

Using No. 7 needles and grey, cast on 140 sts and work in single rib for 8in. Bind off loosely.

Finishing

Join with flat seams throughout. Stitch shoulder seams first, then open out the body and pin the sleeves into position, taking care not to bunch them. Attach the sleeves, then work the side and sleeve seams.

Attach the collar with the bound-off edge to the neckline. Cross over and slip st along front of neck as shown in the illustration opposite.

COCOON-SHAPED COAT

Materials
Yarnworks mohair – 33oz.
1 pair of raglan shoulder pads.

Needles
One pair of No. 7 and one pair of No. 8 needles.

Gauge
Using No. 8 needles and measured over st st, 18 sts and 24 rows = 4in square.

A full-length, edge-to-edge, coat that envelopes the wearer like a cocoon. Knitted entirely in stockinette stitch, it has deep raglan sleeves and turn-back cuffs. This one-size garment fits sizes 12-16 (*see* chart for actual measurements).

Back
Using No. 8 needles, cast on 126 sts and work in st st for 17¾in, ending with an RS row.
Shape raglan: bind off 2 sts at beg of next 2 rows. Next row: purl. Row 2: * k2, sl1, k1, psso, k to last 4 sts, k2 tog, k2.* Keep repeating these 2 rows until 28 sts remain.
Next row: ** p2, p2 tog, p to last 3 sts, sl the last worked st back on to LH needle. Lift the 2nd st on LH needle over it and then replace it on the RH needle, p2.** Row 2: work from * to *. Repeat these last 2 rows until 20 sts remain. Bind off.

Left front
Using No. 8 needles, cast on 9 sts and k 1 row. Cast on 6 sts at beg of next row and p to end. Repeat these last 2 rows 3 times more (33 sts). Cont shaping the front edge by inc 1 st on every row until you have 56 sts. Now inc 1 st at this edge on every alt row until you have 64 sts and then on every 4th row until you have 66

sts. Work straight until the front measures 17¾in, ending on a WS row.
Shape raglan: bind off 2 sts, k to end. Next row: purl. Row 2: k2, sl1, k1, psso, k to end. Keep repeating these 2 rows. When work measures 21in, **shape neck** (meanwhile, cont to shape raglan as before). Dec 1 st at neck edge on next and every following 6th row until 13 decs have been made in all. Now work the neck edge straight and cont to shape the raglan as before until 4 sts remain. Now dec 1 st at raglan edge on every row until 1 st remains. Fasten off.

Right front
Work as for the left front, reversing shapings, working k2 tog instead of sl1, k1, psso.

Sleeves
Using No. 8 needles, cast on 80 sts.
K 1 row and p 1 row, then work in pattern as follows:
Row 1 (RS): knit. Row 2: purl. Repeat these 2 rows 4 times more.
Row 11: purl. Row 12: knit. Repeat these 2 rows 5 times more. Repeat these 22 rows, inc 1 st each end of every 5th row (88 sts).
Row 23 (RS): knit. Cont in st st, inc 1 st each end of every alt row until you have 114 sts. Now inc 1 st each end of every row until you have 130 sts, ending on a WS row. **Shape raglan**: as for back until 44 sts remain.
Next row (WS): work from ** to **. Row 2: work from * to *. Keep repeating these 2 rows until 10 sts remain. Bind off.

Collar
(Worked in two pieces).
Using No. 7 needles, cast on 260 sts.
Row 1 (WS): knit. Row 2: purl. Repeat these 2 rows 4 times more.
Row 11: purl. Row 12: knit. Repeat these 2 rows 3 times more.
Now repeat these 18 rows twice more and then repeat rows 1-10 inclusive. Bind off loosely, using a larger needle. Work a second piece to match.

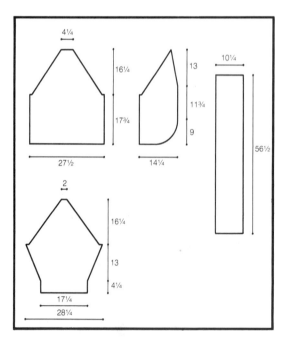

Finishing

Join the sleeve and side seams with a flat seam, remembering that the sleeves have turned-back cuffs so that the WS should be the neat side. Join the side edges of the collar pieces together so that they form a circle. These two seams should be positioned one at the center-back neck and one at the center-back hem. Attach the collar to the coat by the bound-off edge. Pin the right sides tog (the outer edge of the collar must curl under itself), easing it around the curves of the fronts. Sew with a flat seam.

CORSAGE BOLERO

A taste of Fifties glamour with this one-size bolero in black with a jewel-colored mock corsage, using clusters of bobbles. Worked in two pieces with a seam down the center line of the back, the main knitting is stockinette stitch, worked horizontally from the cuff edge, with a garter stitch border added afterwards.

Materials
Yarnworks mohair – black: 12oz; corsage colors (royal blue, fuchsia, bright purple, misty purple and leaf green): less than 1oz of each.
Needles
One pair of No. 8 and one pair of No. 9 needles.
Gauge
Using No. 9 needles and measured over st st, 18 sts and 24 rows = 4in square.

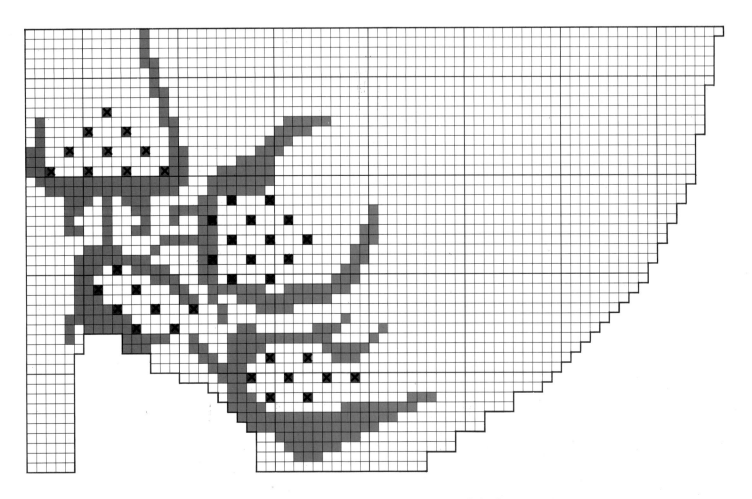

Incorporate the above chart into the pattern for the left front and the back. Where an "X" is shown on the chart, make a bobble in the appropriate color (*see* Techniques, page 12).

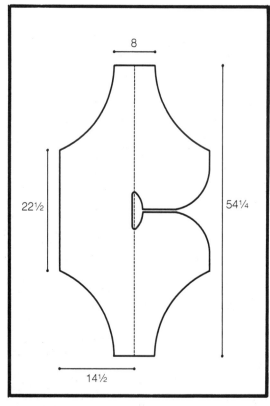

Right front and back

Using No. 8 needles and black, cast on 36 sts and work 5 rows in garter st (k every row). Change to No. 9 needles and cont in st st, inc 1 st each end of next and every following 4th row until you have 48 sts. Now inc 1 st each end of every 3rd row until you have 68 sts. Cont by inc 1 st each end of every alt row until you have 90 sts and then every row until you have 122 sts.

Cast on 3 sts at beg of next 4 rows. Work straight for 5 rows. ** Now dec 1 st at front edge, 2 sts in from the edge, on next and every following 5th row, 5 times in all. Now dec 1 st at this edge on every alt row, 5 times in all. Cont by dec 1 st at this edge on every row until 120 sts remain.

Shape neck: next row (RS): k2, k2 tog, k46, bind off 4 sts, k to end. Cont with back sts only, leaving the front sts on a holder. Dec 1 st at neck edge on next knit row, then work straight for 17 rows. Leave sts on a holder. Return to front sts, joining in yarn at neck edge.

Row 1: bind off 3 sts, p to last 4 sts, p2 tog, p2.
Row 2: k2, k2 tog, k to end. Repeat these 2 rows once more, then row 1 once more (35 sts).

46

Next row: bind off 3 sts, k to last 4 sts, k2 tog, k2. Row 2: p2, p2 tog, p to end. Repeat these 2 rows once more, then the first of them once more (21 sts). Now work neck edge straight and bind off 3 sts at beg of next RS row. Work 1 row straight and bind off, keeping the bind-off gauge the same as the main work.

Left front and back

As for right front, reversing out the shaping and working as far as **. Now dec 1 st at front edge on next and following 5th row, then start working from the chart. Meanwhile, cont to shape as for other side.

Border

Using No. 8 needles and black, cast on 6 sts and work in garter st until the border is long enough to reach from the center back seam, around the bottom edge of the right back, up around the front to the edge of the neck shaping. Pin this to make sure that it does fit, allowing the band to ease around the curves of the front without pulling. **Mitre the corner**: next row: k to last st, turn and k to end. Row 3: k to last 2 sts, turn and k to end. Cont as set, leaving an extra unworked st on every RS row until only 1 st is being worked. Now knit across all sts and cont working straight until the border is long enough to reach around the neck to the other front edge. Work another mitred corner and then work straight until this side of the border reaches to the back center seam. Bind off.

Finishing

Knit the center back seam tog (*see* Techniques, page 17). Join the sleeve and side seams with a flat seam. Join the ends of the border tog with a flat seam, then carefully pin it into position, ensuring that it is evenly distributed. Attach with a flat seam.

COWL-NECKED DOLMAN SWEATER

This very simple, quick to knit sweater comes in two lengths. The longer version looks attractive when worn as a dress over leggings. The generous sleeves make the shorter version ideal for dressier occasions. The body of the jumper is knitted as one piece.

Materials
Yarnworks mohair – 16oz
for long version;
14oz for short version.
Needles
One pair of No. 9 and one
pair of No. 11 needles.
Gauge
Using No. 11 needles and
measured over st st, 12 sts
and 12 rows = 4in square.

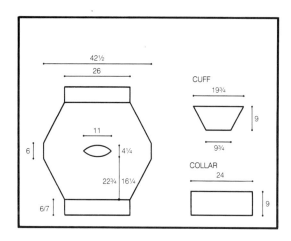

LONG VERSION

Front and back

Using No. 9 needles, cast on 60 sts and work in k1, p1 rib for * 7in. Change to No. 11 needles and, starting with a knit row, work in st st, inc 1 st each end of every alt row until you have 130 sts on your needle. Work 19 rows without shaping (you should finish on a purl row).

Shape neck: k50. Place these sts on a spare needle, bind off center 30 sts, k50. Working on these last 50 sts only, p to last 2 sts, p2 tog. Next row: k2 tog, k to end. Next row: p to last st, inc 1 st. Next row: inc 1, k to end. Next row: p back to neck edge, turn, cast on 30 sts, break off yarn.
Rejoin yarn at neck edge of sts held on spare needle and work as follows: p2 tog, p to end. Next row: k to last 2 sts, k2 tog. Next row: inc

1, p to end. Next row: k to last st, inc 1. Next row: purl. Knit across the 130 sts on both needles. Cont down the back exactly as you have worked the front, but decreasing where you have increased until you have 60 sts ** on your needle. Change to No. 9 needles and k1, p1 rib for 7in. Bind off very loosely.

Collar

Using No. 11 needles, cast on 74 sts. K1, p1 rib until work measures 9in. Bind off very loosely.

Cuffs

Using No. 9 needles, cast on 36 sts. Work in k1, p1 rib until work measures 2in. Inc 1 st each end of next and every alternate row until you have 56 sts. Bind off.

Finishing

Using flat seams, join side and cuff seams and join short ends of neckband. Stitch cuffs into place and sew on neckband, making sure that the seam is at the center back.

SHORT VERSION

Work as for long version to *. Rib for 4¾in. Next row: inc 1, rib 2, rep to end, inc 1 (82 sts). Change to No. 11 needles and cont as for back to **. Change to No. 9 needles and work one row as follows using k1, p1 rib: k2 tog, p1, k1. Repeat to end, k2 tog. Rib for 4¾in. Bind off loosely in ribbing. Complete jumper as for long version.

ZEBRA WAISTCOAT

A stylish, long-line waistcoat in a zebra print, worked in two sizes using the fairisle method.

Back
Using No. 7 needles and black, cast on 78/86 sts. K1, p1 rib for 6 rows. Change to No. 9 needles and white and begin following the chart, working in st st and starting with a knit row. Cont working from the chart until work measures 20in, ending with a purl row. **Shape armholes**: bind off 5/7 sts at beg of next 2 rows. Dec 1 st at each end of next 3 rows, then 1 st at each end of every alt row until 58/62 sts remain. Cont without further shaping until armhole measures 9½in, ending with a purl row. Bind off.

Left front
Using No. 7 needles and black, cast on 39/43 sts and work 6 rows in k1, p1 rib as for back. Change to No. 9 needles and follow chart as indicated for left front. Cont until work measures 17in from beg, ending with a purl row.

Shape front: dec 1 st at end (neck edge) of next row and every following 4th row, 9 times. *At the same time*, when work measures 20in (ending with a purl row), **shape armhole**: bind off 5/7 sts at beg of next row, then dec 1 st at armhole edge at beg of next 3 rows and the following 2 alt rows (20/22 sts). Cont as for back until front matches back to shoulder, ending at armhole edge. Bind off.

Materials
Yarnworks mohair – 6oz black; 6oz white. 6 black buttons.
Needles
One pair of No. 7 and one pair of No. 9 needles.
Gauge
Using No. 9 needles and measured over st st, 16 sts and 20 rows = 4in square.

The chart below should be used for the back and both the left and right fronts.

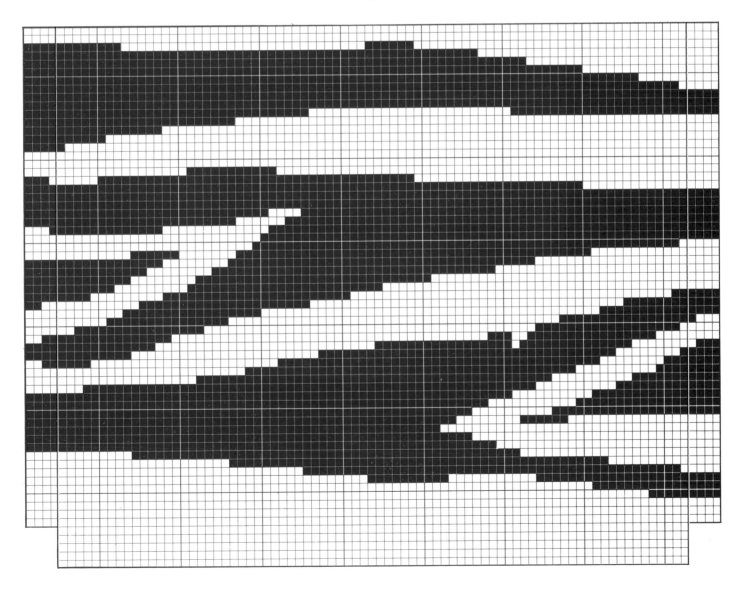

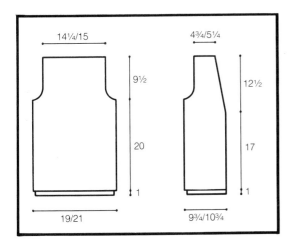

14¼/15 4¾/5¼

9½ 12½

20 17

1 1

19/21 9¾/10¾

Right front
Work as for left front, reversing shapings, reading the chart as indicated for right front.

Front band
Join shoulder seams. Mark left front edge with pins to indicate button placement. Place the first button in the 4th row of rib and the last one level with beg of front shaping. Space the 4 remaining buttons equally in between. Using No. 7 needles and white, cast on 8 sts. Work 2 rows in k1, p1 rib. Next row (buttonhole): rib 3, bind off 2, rib to end. Next row: rib 3, cast on 2, rib to end. Cont in rib, working 5 more buttonholes at pin positions. Cont until band fits all round front edges when slightly stretched. Bind off in ribbing. Backstitch shoulder seams together.

Armbands
With RS of work facing and using No. 7 needles and white, pick up 50 sts evenly around armhole edge. Work 5 rows in k1, p1 rib. Bind off in ribbing.

Finishing
Using flat seams, join side and armband seams. Sew on band and buttons.

CLASSIC CREW-NECK AND V-NECK SWEATER AND CARDIGAN

Materials
Yarnworks mohair – all styles 14/16/16oz; crew neck sweater and crew neck cardigan: 6 buttons; V-neck sweater and V-neck cardigan: 4 buttons.
Needles
One pair of No. 6 and one pair of No. 8 needles.
Gauge
Using No. 8 needles and measured over st st, 18 sts and 24 rows = 4in square.

A combination of classic shapes that may be dressy or casual according to the outfit. The simplicity of the design makes them essential basics for any wardrobe. The crew-neck styles have set sleeves while the V-necks combine with a raglan-sleeve shape. The sizing is a standard women's small/medium/large, the instructions being specified in that order.

CREW-NECK SWEATER

Back
Using No. 6 needles, cast on 82/86/90 sts.
Row 1: * k1, p1, rep from * to end. This row forms single rib. Work in exactly the same way wherever rib is required within the instructions. Rib for 2½in, ending with a WS row. Next row: knit, inc into every 20th st (86/90/94 sts). Now change to No. 8 needles and cont in st st until work measures 15/15½/15¾in.
Shape armholes: bind off 2 sts at beg of next 2 rows. Now dec 1 st each end of every row until 70/72/74 sts remain. Work straight until work measures 21¾/22½/23¼in from the beg, ending with a WS row. **Shape neck and shoulders**: next row: k 20 sts, bind off 30/32/34 sts, k to last 6 sts, turn and p to neck edge. Cont with this set of sts, leaving the others on a holder.

Row 3: k to last 13 sts, turn. Row 4: purl.
Put sts on to a holder and return to the other set. Join in yarn at neck edge, p to last 6 sts, turn and k to end. Row 3: p to last 13 sts, turn. Row 4: knit. Leave sts on a holder.

Front
As for back until work measures 18½/19¼/20in, ending with a WS row. **Shape neck**: next row: k 28/29/30 sts, bind off 14 sts, k to end. Cont with this last set of sts, leaving the others on a holder. Dec 1 st at neck edge on every row until 20 sts remain. Now work straight until work measures 21¾/22½/23¼in, ending on a WS row.
Shape shoulder: next row: k to last 6 sts, turn and p to end. Row 3: k to last 13 sts, turn. Row 4: purl.
Leave sts on a holder and return to the other side of the neck, joining yarn at neck edge. Work as for first side, reversing shapings. Leave sts on a holder.

Sleeves
Using No. 6 needles, cast on 34/36/38 sts and work in single rib for 2in. Change to No. 8 needles and cont in st st, inc 1 st each end of next and every following 6th row, until you have 62/66/70 sts. Now work straight until the sleeve measures 17/17¾/18½in from beg.
Shape sleeve cap: bind off 2 sts at beg of next 2 rows. Then dec 1 st each end of every row until 46/48/50 sts remain. Now dec 1 st each end of every alt row until 36/38/40 sts remain. Then dec 1 st each end of every row until you have 26 sts left. Bind off 4 sts at beg of next 4 rows. Bind off remaining sts.

Neckband
Knit the right shoulder seam tog (*see Techniques, page 17*). Using No. 6 needles and with RS facing, knit up 16/17/18 sts down the left side of the neck, 14 across the front, 16/17/18 sts up the other side and 34/36/38 sts around the back neck (80/84/88 sts). Purl the first row and then cont in single rib until it is 1¼in deep. Bind off in ribbing.

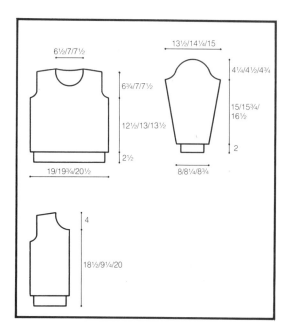

CREW-NECK CARDIGAN

Back and sleeves
As for the sweater.

Right front
Using No. 6 needles, cast on 46/48/50 sts and work in single rib for 2 rows.
Row 3: rib 2, bind off 2, rib to end. Row 4: rib, casting on 2 sts immediately above those bound off on the previous row. Cont until rib measures 2½in, ending with a WS row.
Next row: rib 6 sts and leave these on a pin (they will be worked to form the front band later), k to end, inc into every 20th st (42/44/46 sts on working needle). Change to No. 8 needles and cont in st st until the work measures 15/15½/15¾in from the beg, ending on an RS row.
Shape armhole: bind off 2 sts at beg of next row. Now dec 1 st at armhole edge on every row until 34/35/36 sts remain. Now work straight until the work measures 18½/19¼/20in, ending with a WS row.

Shape neck: bind off 6 sts at beg of next row. Now dec 1 st at neck edge until 20 sts remain. Work straight until work measures 21¾/22½/23¼in from beg, ending with a WS row.
Shape shoulder: as for sweater front.

Left front
As for right front, reversing shapings and omitting the buttonhole.

Buttonband
Slip the 6 held sts from the left front on to a No. 6 needle and cont in single rib as set until the band is long enough to reach the bound-off edge at the front of the neck when very slightly stretched, ending with a WS row. Leave on a pin again. Using safety-pins, mark the button positions, spacing 4 equally between the level of the bottom buttonhole and the one that will be worked at the very top of the neckband. Slip the 6 held sts from the buttonhole band on to a No. 6 needle and work this to match the buttonband, working a buttonhole to correspond with each marker pin. When it is the required length, ending with a WS row, leave the sts on a pin.

Neckband
Knit both shoulder seams tog (*see* Techniques, page 17). Place the buttonhole band sts on to a No. 6 needle and rib across them. Then knit up 22/23/24 sts up the right side of neck, 34/36/38 sts around the back neck and 22/23/24 sts down the left side of neck, finishing by ribbing across the 6 buttonband sts (90/94/98 sts). Work in single rib for 4 rows. On the next 2 rows, work a buttonhole to correspond with those already worked. Rib 2 more rows. Bind off in ribbing.

V-NECK SWEATER

Back
As for the crew-neck sweater until the work measures 11½/12¼/13in.
Shape raglan: bind off 2 sts at beg of next 2 rows. Now dec 1 st each end of next and every following alt row until 24 sts remain. Leave sts on a holder.

Front
As for back until 70/74/78 sts remain. **Divide for neck**: (cont to shape raglan as before throughout), work 35/37/39 sts and turn work, leaving remaining sts on a holder. Dec 1 st at the neck edge on the next and every following 3rd row until 11 decs have been made at this edge. Now work this edge straight and cont

with raglan shaping until 2 sts remain. Work 3 rows straight, work 2 sts tog and fasten off. Return to the other side of the neck, joining in yarn at neck edge. Shape to match the first side.

Sleeves

Using No. 6 needles, cast on 34/36/38 sts and work in single rib for 2½in, ending with a WS row. Next row: knit, inc into every 5th/6th/6th st (40/42/44 sts). Change to No. 8 needles and cont in st st, inc 1 st each end of every 5th row until you have 74/78/82 sts. Work straight until the sleeve measures 17/17¾/18½in from beg when measured on the straight. **Shape raglan:** bind off 2 sts at beg of next 2 rows. Now dec 1 st each end of every row until 62/68/74 sts remain. Now dec 1 st each end of every alt row until 8/8/10 sts remain. Bind off.

Neckband

Using a flat seam, join all raglan seams except that at the back of the right sleeve. Using a No. 6 needle and with RS facing, slip the back neck sts on to the needle and knit up 50/54/58 sts down the left sleeve top and side of neck, 1 axial st from the central loop where the front sts were divided and 50/54/58 sts up the other side of neck and across the sleeve top (125/133/141 sts). Purl the first row and then cont in single rib, working 2 sts tog either side of the axial st (which remains in st st throughout), keeping in rib pattern. When rib measures 1¼in, bind off in ribbing.

V-NECK CARDIGAN

Back and sleeves

As for the V-neck sweater.

Right front

As for right front of the crew-neck cardigan until the work measures 11½/12¼/13in, ending with an RS row.
Shape raglan: bind off 2 sts at beg of next row. Now dec 1 st at this edge on every alt row while dec 1 st on next and every following 4th row at neck edge. When 10 decs have been made at the neck edge, work this edge straight while cont to work raglan shapings until 2 sts remain. Work 2 rows straight. Work 2 tog and fasten off.

Left front

As for left front of crew-neck cardigan until the work measures 11½/12¼/13in, ending with a WS row. Now cont as for right front of the V-neck cardigan, reversing shapings.

Bands

Slip the held sts from the buttonband on to a No. 6 needle and cont in single rib as set until the band is long enough to reach the center of the neck at the back when very slightly stretched. Leave sts on a pin. Using safety-pins, mark the positions of the top and bottom buttons to correspond to the start of the neck shaping on the front and the bottom buttonhole made on the buttonhole band. Divide the band into three between these points and mark the positions of the other 2

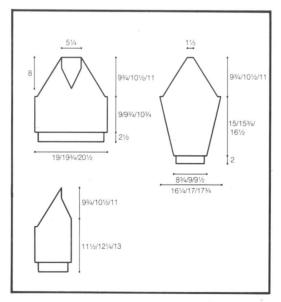

buttons. Work the buttonhole band to match, working the buttonholes to correspond with the button markers. When this band is long enough, knit the bands together (*see* Techniques, page 17).

Finishing
The seams throughout are flat seams.
Crew-neck sweater: knit second shoulder seam tog and join the neckband with a flat seam. Join the side and sleeve seams first and then set sleeves into the armholes.
Crew-neck cardigan: attach the front bands with a very neat flat seam. Attach buttons to marked positions.
V-neck sweater: join the final raglan seam and neckband seam. Join side and sleeve seams.
V-neck cardigan: join raglan, side and sleeve seams. Attach the bands with a very neat flat seam, taking care that the top buttonhole comes no higher than the start of the neck shaping and that the knitted seam of the bands sits dead center of the back neck. Attach buttons to marked positions.

GEOMETRIC SPORTS SWEATER

A bold geometric man's sweater with a criss-cross design, worked using the intarsia method. Ideal for skiing and cross-country jaunts.

Materials
Yarnworks mohair – 15oz main color "A"; 1oz each of contrasting colors "B" and "C".
Needles
One pair of No. 7 and one pair of No. 10 needles.
Gauge
Using No. 10 needles and measured over st st, 16 sts and 18 rows = 4in square.

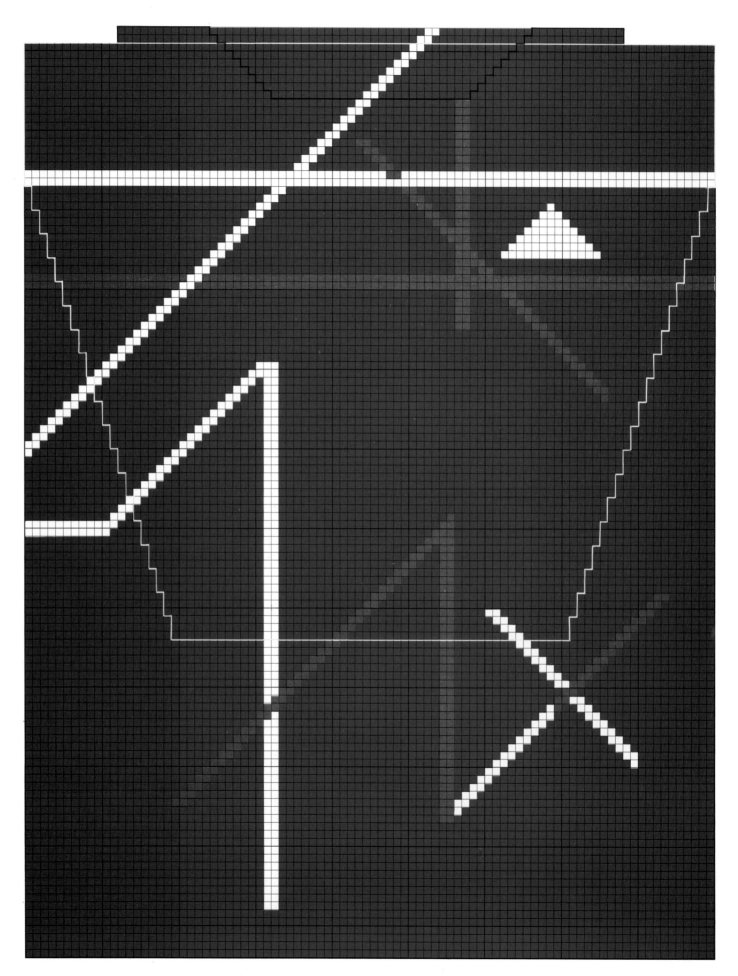

The chart opposite (page 64) should be incorporated into both the back and the front of the sweater. Use the area outlined in yellow for the sleeves.

Front

Using No. 7 needles and color "A", cast on 74 sts. K1, p1 rib for 2 rows, change to "B", rib 2 rows, change to "A", rib 2 rows, change to "C", rib 2 rows, change to "A", rib 10 rows. Next row: in color "A" inc in first st and in every 4th st to end (90 sts). Change to No. 10 needles and, beginning with a knit row, follow the chart until 108 rows have been worked. **Shape neck**: row 109: k32 sts. Place these on a stitch holder, bind off center 26 sts, k32. Cont on the last set of sts only, dec 1 st at neck edge every row until you have 26 sts. **Shape shoulder**: still dec at neck edge, bind off 12 sts at beg of next row and following alt row. Return to held sts, join in yarn at neck edge and work the other side of the neck, reversing shapings.

Back

Work as for front, ignoring the neck shaping.

Sleeves

With No. 7 needles and color "A", cast on 36 sts. Work 2 rows in k1, p1 rib. Change to "B", work 2 rows in rib. Change to "A", work 2 rows in rib. Change to "C", work 2 rows in rib. Change to "A", work 10 rows in rib, inc 16 sts evenly along last row (52 sts). Change to No. 10 needles and begin following chart in st st, inc 1 st each end of every 3rd row until you have 90 sts. Complete the chart without further shaping. Bind off loosely.

Neckband

Join left shoulder seam. Using No. 7 needles and RS of work facing, use color "A" and pick up and knit 6 sts down right front side; 26 sts front neck; 6 sts up left side neck; 42 sts across back. K1, p1 rib for 3 rows in "A", 2 rows in "B", 2 rows in "C" and 3 rows in "A". Bind off loosely. Turn neckband inwards on itself and slip st the bound-off edge to the pick-up edge.

Finishing

Backstitch shoulder seams, then, using flat seams throughout, join sleeves to body and join sleeve seams and side seams together.

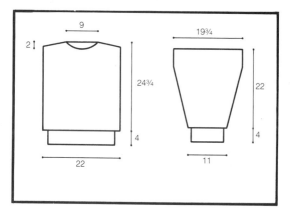

JACKET WITH COLLAR/HOOD

An oversized raglan jacket, styled to take raglan shoulder pads. The tie-belt sits low on the waist and the shoulder-swathing collar doubles as a hood. The ridges of the hood are echoed in the tie-belt and cuffs. The one size fits sizes 10-12.

Materials
Yarnworks mohair – 27oz.
1 pair of raglan shoulder pads.
Needles
One pair of No. 7 and one pair of No. 8 and one pair of No. 9 needles.
Gauge
Using No. 8 needles and measured over st st, 18 sts and 24 rows = 4in square.

Pattern

Row 1 (RS): purl. Row 2: knit. Repeat these two rows 4 times more.
Row 11: knit. Row 12: purl. Repeat these 2 rows 4 times more.
These 20 rows form the ridge pattern of alternate bands of st st and rev st st.

Back

Using No. 7 needles, cast on 86 sts and work in pattern for 30 rows. Now change to No. 8 needles and work in st st, inc 1 st each end of every 3rd row until you have 104 sts. Work 2 rows straight.
Shape raglan: bind off 2 sts at the beg of next 2 rows. * Next RS row: k2, sl1, k1, psso, k to last 4 sts, k2 tog, k2. Row 2: purl.* Keep repeating these 2 rows until 20 sts remain. Work 1 row straight, then bind off loosely.

Left front

Using No. 7 needles, cast on 46 sts and work in pattern for 30 rows. Change to No. 8 needles and cont in st st, inc 1 st at the side edge on every 3rd row until you have 55 sts. Work 2 rows straight.
Shape raglan: next RS row: bind off 2 sts, work to end. Row 2: purl. Row 3: k2, sl 1, k1, psso, k to end. Keep repeating these 2 rows until 50 sts remain. Cont to shape raglan as set, but meanwhile **shape neck**: place a marker at the

front edge and dec 1 st at this edge on next and every following 6th row until 11 decs have been made at this edge in all. Now work this edge straight but cont with raglan shaping until 2 sts remain. Work these tog and fasten off.

Right front

Work as for left front, reversing shapings.

Sleeves

Using No. 7 needles, cast on 52 sts. Work 10 rows in pattern. Change to No. 8 needles and cont in pattern for another 20 rows. Now start working in st st, inc 1 st each end of every alt row until there are 92 sts and then inc 1 st each end of every row until there are 104 sts. Next WS row: **shape raglan**: bind off 2 sts at beg of next 2 rows. Now work as for back from * to *. Keep repeating these 2 rows until 30 sts remain. Now dec 1 st each end of every row, working the purl rows: p2, p2 tog, work to last 4 sts, p2 tog, p2. When 10 sts remain, work 1 row straight, then bind off loosely.

Collar

Using No. 9 needles, cast on 224 sts and work in pattern, dec 1 st each end of every alt row until 124 sts remain. Now change to No. 8 needles and dec 1 st each end of every row until 112 sts remain. Work across next row, working 2 tog every 5th and 6th sts (94 sts). Cont, dec 1 st each end of every row until 68 sts remain. Work across next row, working 2 tog every 4th and 5th sts (51 sts). Resume dec 1 st each end of every row until 35 sts remain. Work across next row, working 2 tog every 2nd and 3rd sts (24 sts). Cont dec 1 st each end of every row until 18 sts remain (this being a 15th pattern row). Bind off loosely.

Ties

Using No. 7 needles, cast on 46 sts and work in pattern, inc 1 st at beg of 3rd and every following alt row until you have 51 sts. Work 8 rows straight, then dec 1 st at this edge on next and every alt row until 46 sts remain. Work 2 rows straight, then bind off loosely, 1 ½ patterns having been completed. Work another to match, reversing shapings.

Finishing

Join the raglans, side and sleeve seam using a flat seam. Attach the ties, straight edge to front edge of jacket, with a flat seam.

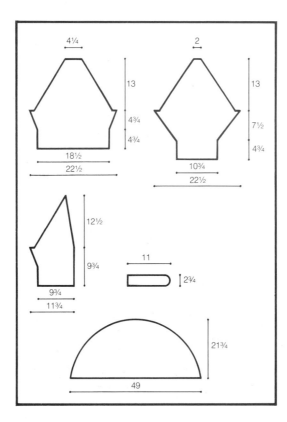

Collar: using a No. 7 needle and with RS facing, knit up 68 sts along one side of the neckline. Distribute them evenly, 5 sts per band (i.e., half pattern), 3 sts for the part band before the bound-off edge. Using a No. 8 needle, bind these sts off, keeping the gauge the same as the work. Repeat this along the other shaped edge. Now pin the collar to the jacket, the shortest edge across the back neck and the shaped edges down the sides of the neck to the point where the neck shaping started. RS of collar facing WS of jacket, sew with a flat seam.

Shoulder pads

Although it is possible to cover foam pads in matching knitted fabric, it is far better to obtain the ready-covered variety with Velcro attached so that the pads may be perfectly positioned.

DROP-SHOULDER DRESS

Materials
Yarnworks mohair – 26oz.
Needles
One pair of No. 6 and one
pair of No. 7 and one pair
of No. 8 needles.
Gauge
Using No. 8 needles and
measured over pattern, 18
sts and 24 rows = 4in
square.

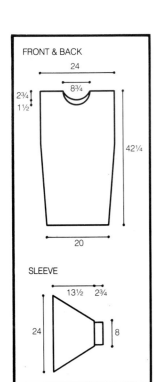

A loose-fitting dress with drop shoulders and
deep round neck. The very wide ribs create a
flattering vertical banding. The one size fits
sizes 8-12 (*see* diagram for actual
measurements).

Back

Using No. 7 needles, cast on 92 sts.
Row 1: * k2, p2, rep from * to end. Keep
repeating this row to form double rib for 1¼in,
ending with a WS row. Change to No. 8
needles and cont in main rib pattern as follows:
Row 1: k1, * p10, k10, rep from * to last 11 sts,
p10, k1. Row 2: p1, * k10, p10, rep from * to last
11 sts, k10, p1. Keep repeating these 2 rows to
form the 10 x 10 rib pattern, inc 1 st each end of
the next and every following 15th row until
you have 104 sts, working all the new sts into
pattern, i.e., a knit band on the RS of work that
will be 6 sts wide either side when the required
no of sts is reached. Now work straight until
the dress measures 39½in.

Shape neck: next row: pattern 42 sts, bind off
20 sts, pattern to end. Cont with this set of sts,
leaving the others on a holder. Keeping in
pattern throughout, dec 1 st at neck edge on
every row until 32 sts remain. Now work
straight until the dress measures 42¼in. Leave
sts on a holder. Return to other side of neck,
joining in yarn at neck edge. Shape to match
first side. Leave sts on a holder.

Front

Work as for back until the dress measures
37¾in.
Shape neck: pattern 44 sts, bind off 16 sts,
pattern to end. Cont with this set of sts,
leaving the others on a holder. Dec 1 st at neck
edge on every row until 38 sts remain, then dec
1 st at neck edge on every alt row until 32 sts
remain. Work straight until work measures
42¼in from beg. Leave sts on a holder. Return
to other side, joining in yarn at neck edge.
Shape to match. Leave sts on a holder.

Left sleeve

(Knitted sideways)
Using No. 8 needles, cast on 3 sts and purl the
1st (RS) row. Knit the next row, inc into the last
st. Cont to work in rev st st, inc 1 st at this edge

until you have 11 sts. Cont inc 1 st at this edge
on every row, but work the next 10 new sts as
st st on the RS of work, to start forming the rib
pattern. Keep inc and bringing new sts into the
10 x 10 rib until you have 61 sts. Now cast on 4
sts at the beg of the next 3 RS rows, working
these 12 sts as a st st band of rib. Work straight
in pattern for 8in.
Cont in pattern, bind off 4 sts at beg of next 3
RS rows. Now dec 1 st at this edge on every
row until 3 sts remain. Bind off.

Right sleeve

As for left sleeve, reversing shapings.

Cuffs

Using No. 6 needles and with RS facing, knit
up 36 sts along the cuff edge of the sleeve and
work in double rib for 2¾in. Bind off.

Neckband

Knit the left shoulder seam tog (*see*
Techniques, page 17). Using No. 6 needles and
with RS facing, knit up 14 down, 20 across and
14 sts up around the back neck and then 22
down, 16 across and 22 sts up around the front
neck (108 sts). Knit the first row, then work in
double rib for 1in. Bind off in rib.

Finishing

Knit the second shoulder seam tog and join
neckband edges with a flat seam. Open body
out and pin sleeves in position, taking great
care not to bunch them. Attach with a flat
seam. Now sew the cuffs with a flat seam and
the sleeve seam with a very narrow backstitch.
Join the sides with a flat seam.

JOAN CRAWFORD COAT

Materials
Yarnworks mohair – 37/39oz. 1 pair of straight-edged shoulder pads.
Needles
One pair of No. 8 needles.
Gauge
Using No. 8 needles and measured over st st, 18 sts and 24 rows = 4in square.

An elegant "fur" coat, re-creating the boxy line of the Forties with padded shoulders and set sleeves. Both body and sleeves are knitted sideways to take advantage of the natural fall of the knitted fabric. Instructions are quoted for sizes 1/2 throughout. Size 1 fits sizes 10-12; size 2 fits sizes 12-14. The diagram makes the garment appear extremely wide since no allowance has been made for the "gathering" effect of the stitch.

Pattern
Row 1 (RS): purl. Row 2: knit. Repeat these 2 rows 4 times more.
Row 11: knit. Row 12: purl.
Repeat these 2 rows 4 times more.
These 20 rows form the ridge pattern of alt bands of st st and rev st st. **NOTE:** Work in pattern throughout unless otherwise instructed.

Back
Using No. 8 needles, cast on 130 sts and work in pattern for 10 rows.
Row 11: k2, inc 1, k to end. Cont to inc 1 st, 2 sts in, at this armhole edge on every row until you have 144 sts. Now cast on 32 sts at beg of next row. Work to end of this row and cont in pattern for 10 more rows, the next row being row 16 of pattern. Row 16: purl to the last 20 sts, turn the work (*see* Techniques, page 13).

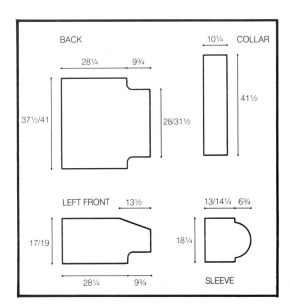

BACK
28¼   9¾
37½/41
28/31½

10¼   COLLAR
41½

LEFT FRONT   13½
17/19
28¼   9¾

13/14¼   6¾
18¼
SLEEVE

Row 17: knit to end. Work 3 more rows normally to complete the pattern.*
Now work 8/9 more complete patterns, turning on the 16th row of each pattern, as described. Cont in pattern without any further turning. Work 4 rows of the next pattern. At beg of next row, **shape armhole:** bind off 32 sts, work to end. Now dec 1 st, 2 sts in from the armhole edge on every row until 130 sts remain and 11/12 complete patterns have been worked. Now work straight for 10 rows. Bind off, keeping the gauge the same as the work.

Left front
Work as for the back until *. Now work 2 more complete patterns, turning on the 16th row of each pattern as before. Work 4/14 more pattern rows. At beg of next row (RS), **shape neck:** bind off 5 sts, work to end. Repeat this on every RS row until 116 sts remain. Work 2 rows straight and then bind off, taking care to keep the bound-off edge gauge the same as the work.

Right front
As for the left front, but reversing all shapings.

Sleeves
Using No. 8 needles, cast on 60/65 sts. Work 10 rows straight.
Shape sleeve cap: on next row, k2, inc 1, k to end. Cont to inc 1 st, 2 sts in from sleeve cap edge, on every row until you have 90/95 sts and 2 complete patterns have been worked. Work straight for 1½ patterns, then dec 1 st, 2 sts in from sleeve head edge on every row until 60/65 sts remain. Work straight until 5½ patterns have been worked. Bind off.

Collar
Worked in st st in 2 pieces.
Using No. 8 needles, cast on 190 sts and work in st st for 10¼in. Bind off loosely. Work another piece to match. Join them end to end with a flat seam to make one long strip.

Finishing
Shoulders: for the purposes of finishing, a "band" refers to half a pattern. By knitting up sts and then knitting them together, the pattern bands may be gently gathered up to

size without becoming bulky. Take the left front, with RS facing, and using No. 8 needles, knit up 24/28 sts across the shoulder line from the sleeve end to the neck edge, dividing into 4 sts across a complete band and 2 sts over a part band. Now take up the back of the coat and knit up exactly the same number of sts across the left shoulder.

Knit the shoulders together as described in Techniques, page 17. Take care to match the bands st for st from front to back. Join the other shoulder seam the same way. Do not break the yarn but continue knitting up 30 sts across the back neck and then bind these sts off.

Side and sleeve seams: join these with a flat seam, taking care to get the side seams absolutely flush at hem point so that the coat will hang properly. Set the sleeves into the armholes with a very narrow backstitch.

Collar: fold the collar in two lengthways, RS (rev st st) facing. Join the hem edges together with a flat seam, then turn the collar right side out. Place the collar on to the coat, RS facing, with the bottom edges fractionally above the hem-line to allow for dropping. Pin these seamed edges to the hem-line and the center seam to the center-back neck. Now divide the remaining fabric equally around the coat, easing a little extra fabric around the neck curves. Stitch down the first layer of the collar with a very narrow backstitch. Now turn the collar under itself and slip st down the other edge, just the far side of the backstitch line. Take great care not to create a twist between the two layers of collar as it will not hang correctly.

Shoulder pads
Although it is possible to cover foam pads in matching knitted fabric, it is far better to obtain the ready-covered variety with Velcro attached so that the pads may be perfectly positioned.

LUCKY JUMPER

An oversized, shawl-collared jumper covered in good-luck charms, worked in stockinette stitch using the intarsia method.

Back
Using No. 7 needles and main color, cast on 86 sts. K1, p1 rib for 6in, inc 14 sts evenly across

Materials
Yarnworks mohair – 18oz of main color; 1oz each of 6 contrasting colors; 1¾oz of lurex ribbon.
Needles
One pair of No. 7 and one pair of No. 9 needles.
Gauge
Using No. 9 needles and measured over st st, 16 sts and 20 rows = 4in square.
Stitches
Use st st throughout except where a circle or an "X" is shown on the charts. On these sts, make a small bobble by knitting 3 sts from one in the color indicated in the circle, then pass the first 2 sts over the 3rd. A circle indicates a yellow bobble; an "X" indicates a pink bobble.

The chart overleaf (page 76) should be incorporated into the back of the sweater, the one on page 77 into the front.

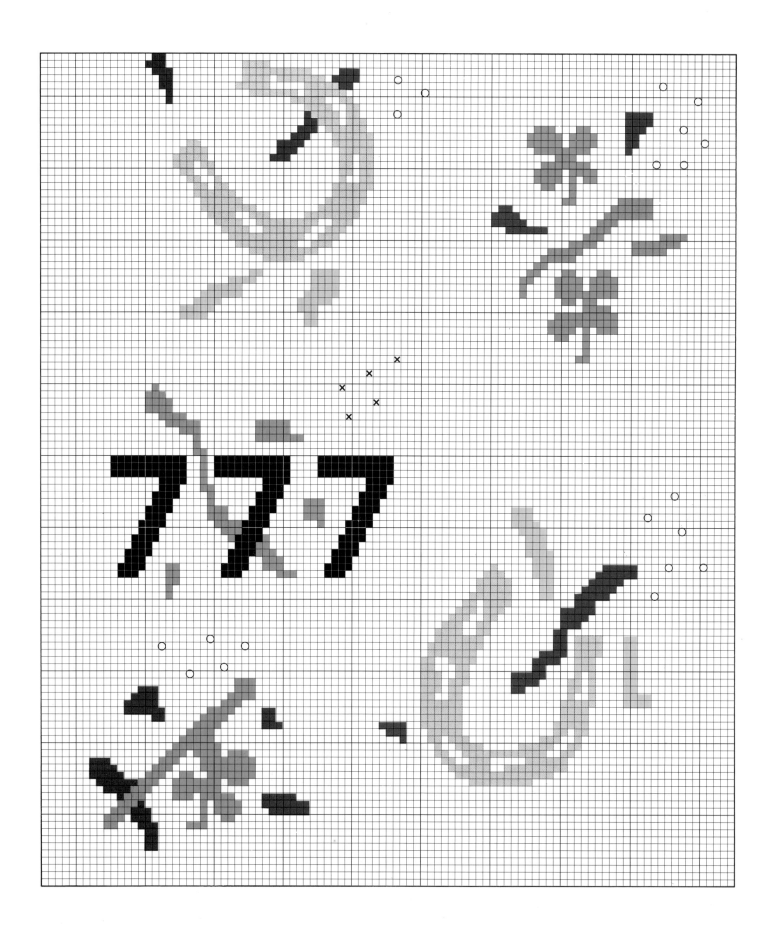

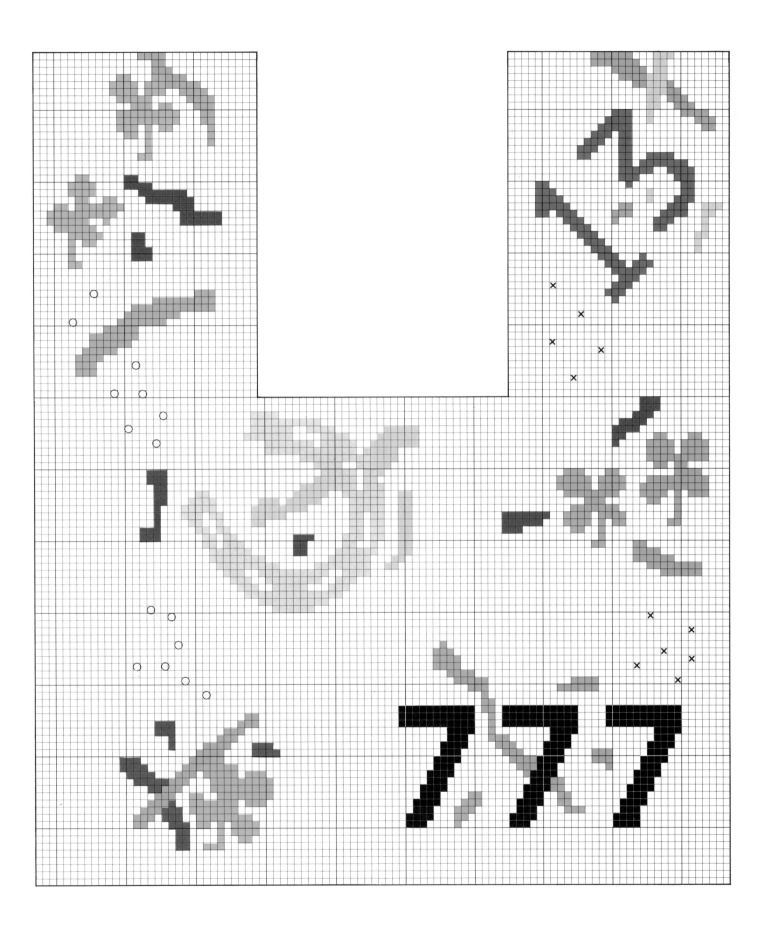

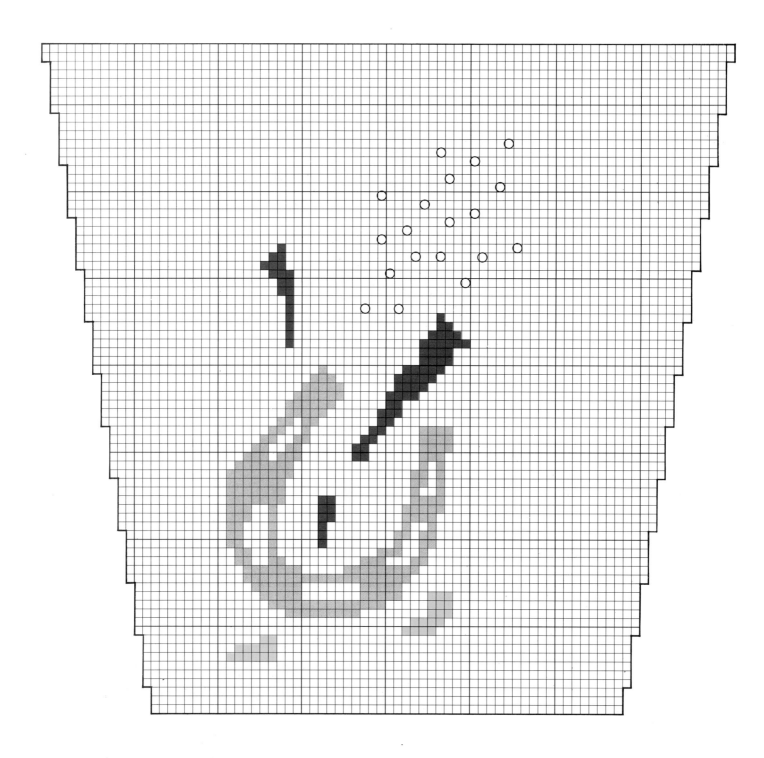

Incorporate the above chart into the left sleeve and the chart opposite (page 79) into the right sleeve.

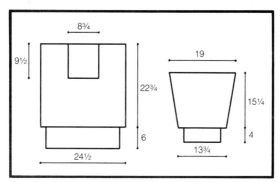

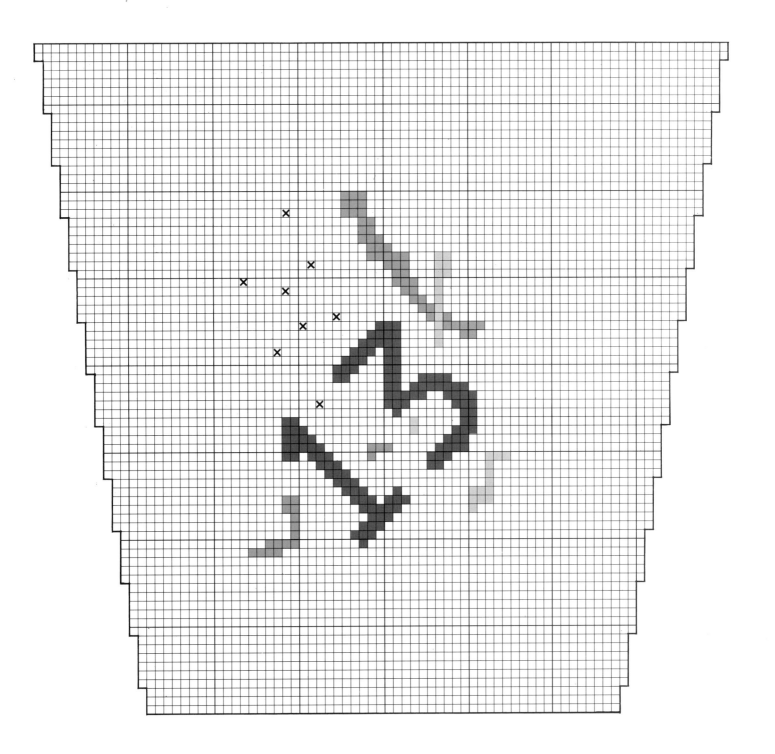

last row of rib (100 sts). Change to No. 9 needles and cont in st st, following chart (page 76) until 121 rows. Row 122: bind off 32 sts, mark with colored thread. Bind off 36 sts, mark again, bind off remaining 32 sts.

Front
Work as for back until row 68. Next row: work 32 sts, bind off center 36 sts. Sl first 32 sts on to a holder, work on last 32 sts only and cont straight on these, following the chart (page 77) until front matches back. Repeat for other side of neck.

Sleeves
Using No. 7 needles with main color, cast on 38 sts. K1, p1 rib for 4in, inc 18 sts evenly across last row of rib (56 sts). Change to No. 9 needles and, following the charts (pages 78 and 79), inc 1 st each end of the 3rd and the 12 following 6th rows (82 sts). Work 2 more rows. Bind off loosely.

Collar
Using No. 7 needles and main color, cast on 138 sts. Work in k1, p1 rib for 9in. Bind off using a No. 9 needle.

Finishing
Match colored threads on back with front inner shoulder edges. Backstitch shoulder seams and, using a flat seam, sew sleeves to body. Join sleeve and side seams. Sew collar into position (*see* illustration, page 40). Sew in all ends securely. Do not knot. Take extra care with the silver ribbon as this tends to fray.

WRAP COAT WITH COWL

A three-quarter length wrap-around coat with a throw over the shoulder, held in place by threading through a crochet chain. There is a hook and loop fastening at the neck under the right front to keep the left front in position. Knitted in stockinette stitch, a moss stitch border prevents curling. The cowl is knitted as a separate piece. The one size fits an 8-10 (*see* diagram for actual measurements).

Back
Using No. 6 needles, cast on 105 sts.
Row 1: k1, * p1, k1, rep from * to end. Keep repeating this row to form moss st. Work 7 rows in all, then change to No. 8 needles and cont in st st until work measures 30¾in, ending with a WS row.
Work neck border: next row: k40, moss st 25, k to end. Row 2: p39, moss st 27, p to end. Keep widening the moss st area, as set, by 1 st each side on every row until 35 sts are being worked in moss st. Leave sts on a spare needle.

Left front
Using No. 6 needles, cast on 50 sts. Work in moss st for 7 rows, inc 1 st at front edge on every row. Now change to No. 8 needles.
Row 8 (WS): moss st 6, p into st below and then st itself (inc made), p to end. Cont working in st st with a 6 st moss st border, inc 1 st in the same position on every row until you have 70 sts. Now work straight, working a 5 st moss st border at the same edge all the way up the front, until the work measures 28in from beg, ending on a WS row.
Work neck border: next row: k47, moss st 11, k7, moss st 5. Row 2: moss st 5, p6, moss st 13, p to end. Row 3: k45, moss st 15, k5, moss st 5. Row 4: moss st 5, p 4, moss st 17, p to end. Row 5: k43, moss st 19, k3, moss st 5. Row 6: moss st 5, p2, moss st 21, p to end. Row 7: k41, moss st 5, bind off 13, moss st to end.
Cont with this set of sts, leaving the others on a holder. Cont in moss st, dec 1 st at neck edge on every row until 8 sts remain. Now dec 1 st at neck edge on every alt row until 5 sts remain. Work straight until work measures 32in from beg, measured on the straight. Bind off. Return to held sts, joining in yarn at neck edge. Maintaining a 5 st moss st border at this edge, dec 1 st on every row until 43 sts remain.

Now dec 1 st at neck edge on every alt row until 40 sts remain. Now work straight, still maintaining the moss st border until the work measures 32in. Leave sts on a spare needle.

Right front
Work as for left front, reversing all shapings until you have 70 sts. Now work a 5 st moss st border as on the other side, but inc inside the border on every alt row until you have 80 sts and then on every 3rd row until you have 110 sts. Now work straight (maintaining border throughout), until the work measures 28in, ending on a WS row.
Work neck border: next row: moss st 5, k47, moss st 11, k to end. Row 2: p46, moss st 13, p46, moss st 5. Row 3: moss st 5, k45, moss st 15, k to end. Row 4: p44, moss st 17, p44, moss st 5. Row 5: moss st 5, k43, moss st 19, k to end. Row 6: p42, moss st 21, p42, moss st 5. Row 7: moss st 5, k41, moss st 5, bind off 11, moss st 5, k to end.

Materials
Yarnworks mohair – 39oz.
1 pair of fur- coat fastenings (loop and hook).
Needles
One pair of No. 6 and one pair of No. 8 needles. One medium crochet hook.
Gauge
Using No. 8 needles and measured over st st, 18 sts and 24 rows = 4in square.

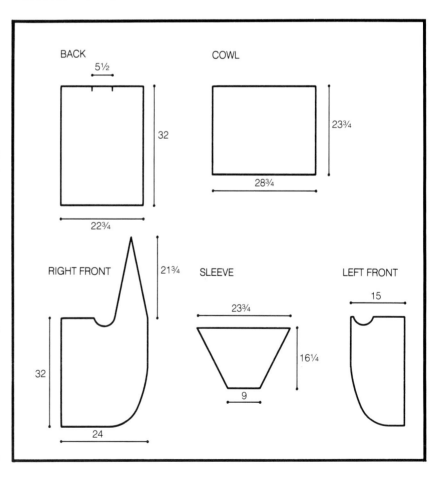

Cont with this set of sts, leaving the others on a holder. Maintaining the moss st border, dec 1 st at neck edge on every alt row until 6 decs have been made in all and 40 sts remain. Work straight until work measures 32in. Leave sts on a holder. Return to other set of sts, joining in yarn at neck edge and shape as for other side (45 sts remain). Now work straight until work measures 32in, maintaining moss st borders at either end of row throughout. Dec 1 st at each end of every following 6th row until 13 sts remain. Now cont entirely in moss st, dec as before, until 3 sts remain. Bind off.

Sleeves

Using No. 6 needles, cast on 43 sts and work in moss st for 7 rows. Change to No. 8 needles and cont in st st, inc 1 st each end of next and every following 4th row, until you have 63 sts. Now inc 1 st each of every alt row until you have 119 sts. Bind off loosely.

Cowl

Using No. 8 needles, cast on 132 sts and work as follows: Row 1 (WS): knit. Row 2: purl. Repeat these 2 rows 5 times more. Row 13: purl. Row 14: knit. Repeat these last 2 rows 4 times more.

These 22 rows form the pattern. Work 6 patterns in all, then repeat rows 1-12 inclusive. Bind off loosely.

Finishing

Knit the left shoulder seam tog (*see* Techniques, page 17), bind off 25 sts for the back neck, then knit the right shoulder seam tog.

Open out the body and pin the sleeves in position, taking care not to bunch them. Attach with a flat seam. Join side and sleeve seams similarly.

Attach the fastening loop to the point where the right shoulder seam meets the neck edge and the fastening hook to the RH side of the left front so that it is not visible from the RS. Crochet a chain (*see* Techniques, page 13), approx 4¼in long and attach this to form a long loop along the left shoulder seam so that the point of the right front may pass through it. Join the side edges, not the cast-on and bound-off edges, of the cowl with a flat seam to form a tube. This is left as a separate item and not attached to the coat.

PEACOCK JUMPER

A bat-wing embroidered and sequinned jumper with a shallow V-neck, knitted in stockinette stitch from cuff to cuff, using the intarsia method. The jumper is knitted in one piece starting with the left cuff.

Materials
Yarnworks mohair – 19oz of main color and 1oz each of turquoise, purple and gold. Turquoise silk embroidery thread; gold lurex thread; gold, turquoise and purple sequins.
Needles
One pair of No. 7 and one pair of No. 9 needles.
Gauge
Using No. 9 needles and measured over st st, 16 sts and 20 rows = 4in square.

The chart on pages 86 and 87 should be incorporated into the back of the jumper.

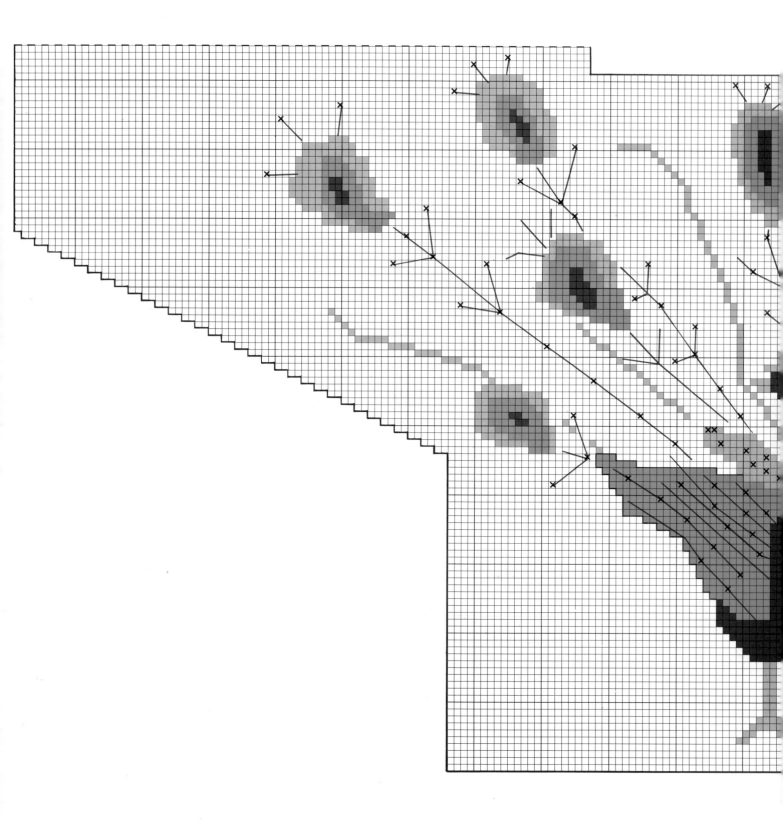

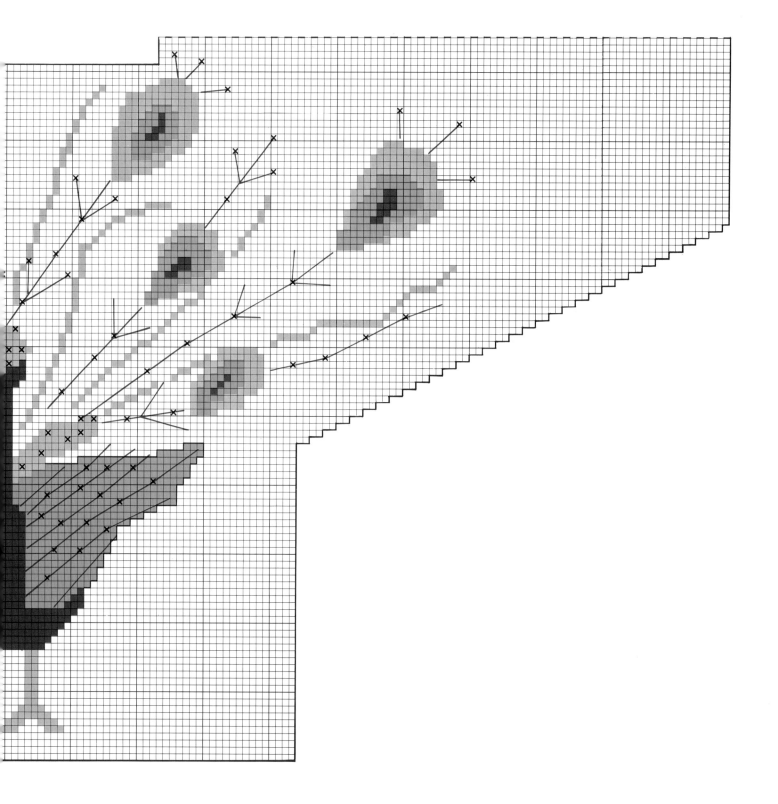

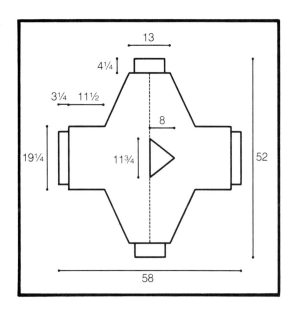

Using No. 7 needles and main color, cast on 32 sts. K1, p1 rib for 4¼in, inc 22 sts evenly along last row of rib. Change to No. 9 needles and, beginning with a knit row, start to follow the chart in st st, inc 1 st at each end of the 1st row and every following alt row until you have 118 sts. Bind on 46 sts at beg of next 2 rows. Work 23 more rows following the chart, then divide for V-neck.

Next row: work pattern over 101 sts, leave these sts on a spare needle for the front. Bind off 5 sts. Work pattern over 104 sts. Cont working on this last set of sts, dec 1 st at neck edge, every row, 28 times. Then inc 1 st at neck edge, every row, 28 times. Cast on 5 sts at neck edge and leave these sts on a spare needle. Go back to the sts held for back and following chart, work 55 rows. Now work across all the sts (front and back) and cont to follow the chart for a further 17 rows. Bind off 46 sts at beg of next 2 rows for the front and back, then begin shaping for sleeve by dec 1 st each end of every alt row until you have 54 sts.

Next row: dec 22 sts evenly along row (32 sts). Change to No. 7 needles and k1, p1 rib for 4¼in. Bind off loosely in ribbing.

Body ribs
With No. 7 needles, pick up 82 sts along the bottom front of jumper. K1, p1 rib for 16 rows, bind off loosely in ribbing. Repeat for back.

Neckband
With a No. 7 circular needle, pick up 35 sts down left side neck, 1 st from center "V" (mark this st with a colored thread), 35 sts from RS. 50 sts across front (121 sts), work 1 row in k1, p1 rib, dec 1 st (by knitting 2 sts tog) either side of the "V". Repeat this row once more, bind off in ribbing.

Embroidery and finishing
Securely sew in loose ends. Using silk embroidery thread and chain st (see Techniques page 18) embroider the feather stems indicated in red on the chart. Using normal sewing thread, sew sequins over the head, upper wings and body, and at the tips of the feathers. Join side seams using a flat seam.

POLKA-DOT SWEATER

Bold black polka-dots and a scoop-necked collar add pazazz to this simple-to-knit sweater worked in stockinette stitch, using the intarsia method.

Materials
Yarnworks mohair – 13oz main color; 3½oz black.
Needles
One pair of No. 7 and one pair of No. 10 needles.
Gauge
Using No. 10 needles and measured over st st, 16 sts and 18 rows = 4in square.

Incorporate the chart opposite (page 91) into both the front and the back.

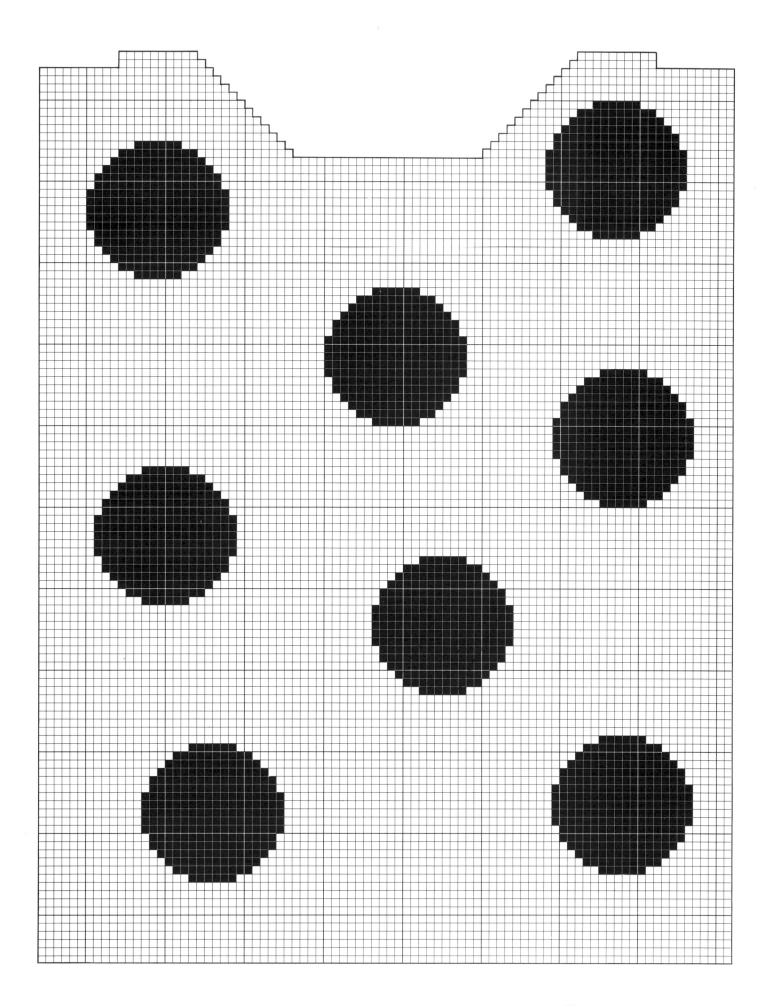

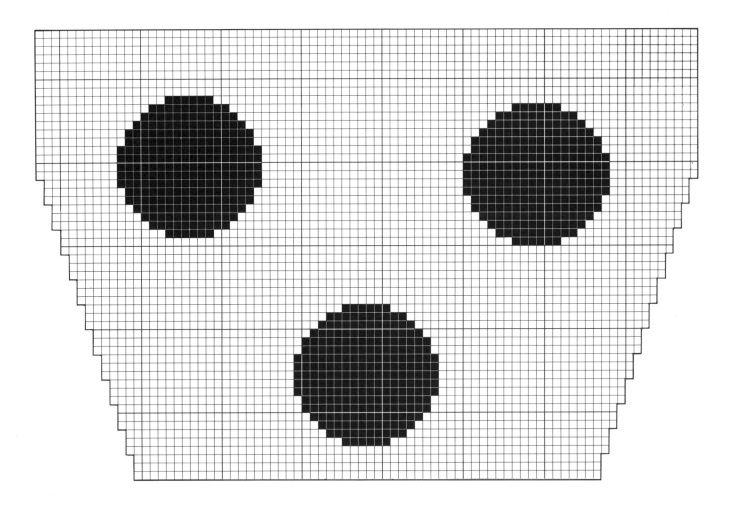

The chart above should be incorporated into both sleeves.

Back and front

Using No. 6 needles and main color, cast on 78 sts. K1, p1 rib for 4in. Inc 10 sts evenly along last row of rib (88 sts). Change to No. 10 needles and, beginning with a knit row, work in st st from the chart until the 90th row has been completed.

Shape neck: cont to follow the chart, work 32 sts, place these sts on a holder, bind off 24 sts, work to end. With this last set of stitches only, dec 1 st at neck edge on the next and the following 10 rows, ending at shoulder edge.

Shape shoulder: next row: bind off 10 sts, pattern to last 2 sts, k2 tog. Next row: p2 tog, p to end. Bind off remaining 10 sts. With WS of work facing, rejoin yarn to remaining sts. P2 tog, work to end, complete to match first side, reversing shaping.

Sleeves

Using No. 7 needles and main color, cast on 40 sts, k1, p1 rib for 4in. Inc 18 sts evenly along last row of rib. Change to No. 10 needles and, beginning with a knit row, follow chart in st st, inc 1 st each end of the 4th row and every following 4th row until you have 82 sts. Work 8 rows without shaping, bind off loosely.

Collar

Using No. 7 needles and main color, cast on 20

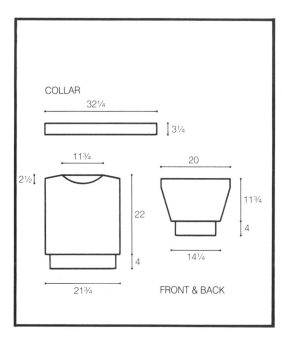

COLLAR

32¼

3¼

11¾

20

2½

22

11¾

4

4

14¼

21¾

FRONT & BACK

sts. K1, p1 rib for 32¼in. Bind off loosely in ribbing.

Finishing
Backstitch shoulder seams. Using a flat seam, join sleeves to main body, matching sleeve tops to shoulder seams. Flat seam side seams. Pin 2 corner edges of the collar to center back of jumper. Sew collar to neck edge along this edge only so that collar has 2 points at the center back.

RIB AND CABLE JUMPER

Materials
Yarnworks mohair – 19oz.
Needles
One pair of No. 8 and one pair of No. 10½ medium-sized cable needles.
Gauge
Using No. 10½ needles and measured over st st, 15 sts and 17 rows = 4in square.

A heavily textured, chunky country jumper in two sizes. The deep raglan makes this jumper suitable for men and women.

Cable rib (CR)

Over 10 sts: rows 1, 3 and 5 (RS): p2, k6, p2. Rows 2, 4 and 6: k2, p6, k2. Row 7: p2, sl next 3 sts on to cable needle and hold at back, k3, then k3 from cable needle, p2. Rows 8, 10 and 12: repeat row 2. Rows 9 and 11: repeat row 1. Rows 13, 15, 17 and 19: p2, k6, p2. Rows 14, 16, 18 and 20: k2, p6, k2. Repeat rows 1-20.

Back

With No. 8 needles, cast on 64 (72) sts and k1, p1 rib for 2¾in, ending with a purl row. Next row: **1st size**: rib 1, *M1, rib 2; rep from * to last 3 sts, M1, rib 3 (95 sts). **2nd size**; rib 1 (M1, p2) twice, *M1, rib 3, M1, rib 2; rep from * to last 2 sts. M1, rib 2 (101 sts). **Both sizes**: change to No. 10½ needles and work in pattern as follows: 1st row (RS): p1, k2, 8/9 times. * K 1st row of CR over next 10 sts, k2, p2, k1, p2, k2. Repeat from * once. K 1st row of CR over next 10 sts. K2, p1, 8/9 times. 2nd row: k1, p2, 8/9 times. *K 2nd row of CR over next 10 sts. P2, k2, p1, k2, p2. Repeat from * once. K 2nd row of CR over next 10 sts. P2, k1, 8/9 times. The pattern is now set, using CR guide. Work pattern until back measures 15¾in, ending with RS facing for next row. **Shape raglans**: bind off 3 sts at beg of next 2 rows. Dec 1 st at each end of next and every alt row until 49/51 sts remain. Work 1 row, dec 1 st at each end of every row until 33/35 sts remain. Leave remaining sts on a spare needle.

Front

Work as for back until 53/55 sts remain in raglan shaping. Work 1 row. **Divide for neck**: work 2 tog, work pattern over 15/16 sts, turn and leave remaining sts on a spare needle. Cont on these 16/17 sts. Dec 1 st at neck edge on next 3 rows. *At the same time* dec 1 st at raglan edge as before 12/13 sts. Dec 1 st at each end of next 2/3 rows, 8/7 sts. Now dec 1 st at raglan edge only on every row until 2 sts remain. Next row: k2 tog and fasten off. With RS facing, sl center 19 sts on a length of yarn. Rejoin yarn to remaining sts, pattern to last 2 sts, work 2 tog. Work to match first side, reversing shapings.

Sleeves

With No. 8 needles, cast on 32/36 sts and work rib as for back for 2¾in, ending with a purl row. Next row: rib 3/4 sts. *M1, rib 1, rep from * to last 3/4 sts. M1, rib to end, 59/65 sts. Change to No. 10½ needles and work in pattern as follows: first row (RS): p1, k2, 2/3 times. * K first row of CR over next 10 sts. K2, p2, k1, p2, k2. Repeat from * once. K first row of CR over next 10 sts. K2, p1, 2/3 times. Cont in pattern as set, inc 1 st at each end of every RS row until there are 77/83 sts, working inc sts into side rib pattern. Now inc 1 st at each end of every following 4th row until there are 89/95 sts, working inc sts into side rib pattern. Work straight until sleeve measures 14½/15in from beg, ending with a WS row.
Shape raglan: bind off 3 sts at beg of next 2 rows. Dec 1 st at each end of next and every alt row until 63/67 sts remain. Work 1 row. Now dec 1 st at each end of every row until 6 sts remain. Leave remaining sts on a safety-pin.

Finishing and neck border

Join raglan with a flat seam, leaving left back raglan open. **Neck border**: with RS facing and No. 8 needles, k6 from left sleeve. Knit up 10 sts down left side of neck, k19 from front, k10 sts up RS of neck, k6 from right sleeve, then 33/35 sts from back, dec 3 sts evenly, 79/81 sts. Work in k1, p1 rib for 4¾in. Using a No. 10½ needle, bind off in ribbing. Join left back raglan and neck border. Fold neck border in half to WS and sew loosely in position. Join side and sleeve seams.

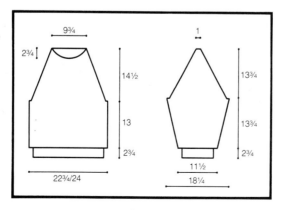

SHIELD CARDIGAN

A jungle print, dropped-sleeve, crew-necked cardigan worked in stockinette stitch, using the intarsia method.

Back
Using No. 7 needles and main color, cast on 70 sts and work in k1, p1 rib for 15 rows.

Materials
Yarnworks mohair – 15oz main color; 1¾oz of each contrasting color.
Needles
One pair of No. 7 and one pair of No. 10 needles.
Gauge
Using No. 10 needles and

The chart overleaf (page 98) should be incorporated into the front of the cardigan, the chart on page 99 into the back. Where an "X" is shown on the chart, make a bobble.

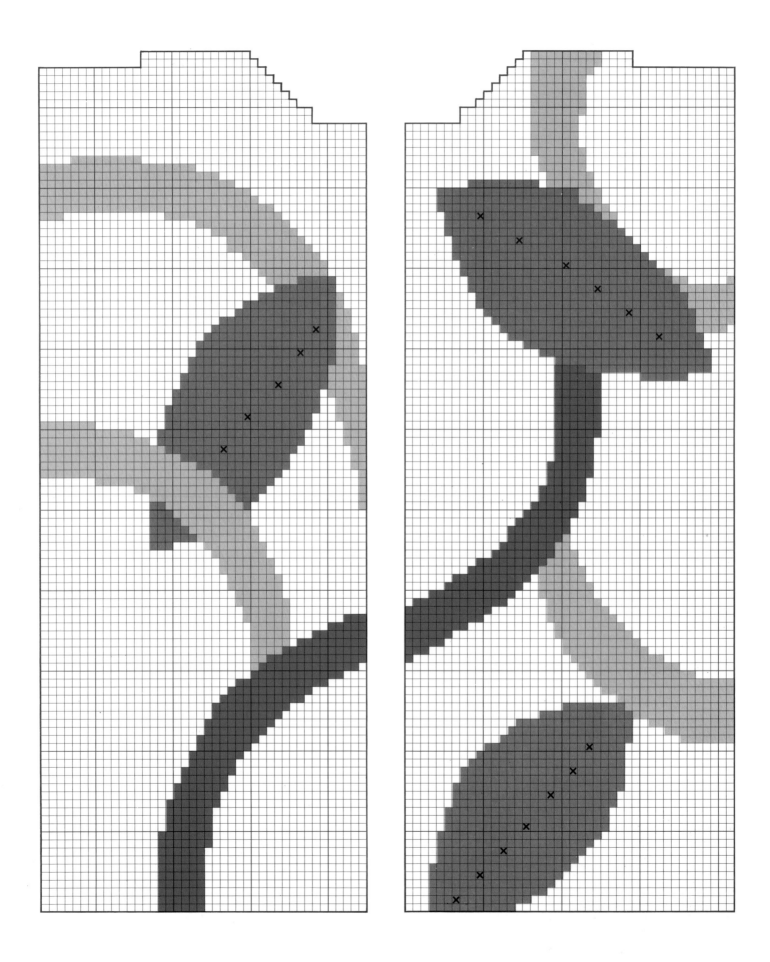

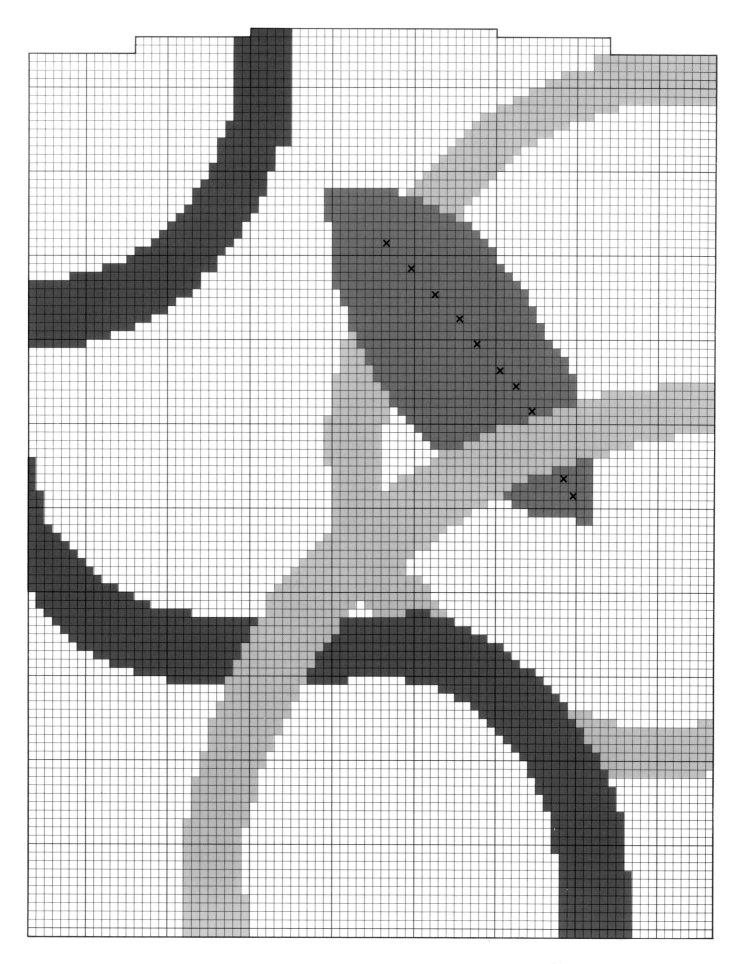

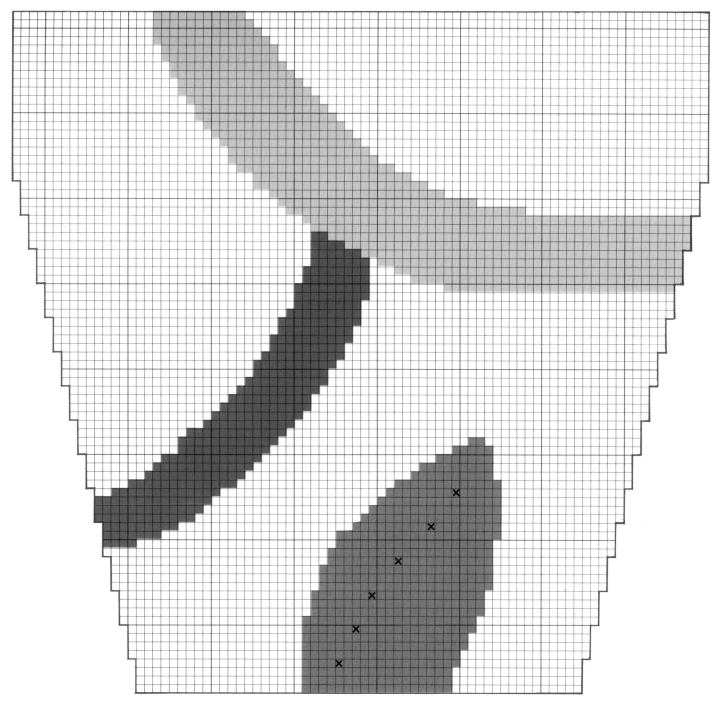

Next row: work in k1, p1 rib, inc 1 st in the first st and every following 5th st (84 sts). Change to No. 10 needles and, beginning with a knit row, follow chart working in st st. Work straight to shoulder shaping. Bind off 13 sts at beg of the next 2 rows. Bind off remaining sts.

Right front

Using No. 7 needles and main color, cast on 36 sts. K1, p1 rib for 15 rows, inc 6 sts evenly across last row (42 sts). Change to No. 10 needles and, beginning with a knit row, follow chart working in st st.

Shape neck: next row: (knit row): bind off 7 sts at beg of row, then 2 sts at beg of next alt row,

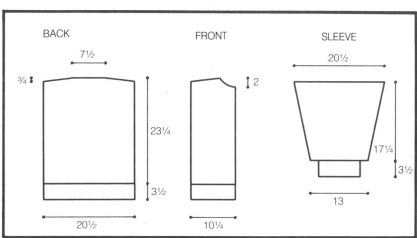

Incorporate the chart on page 101 into the sleeves.

then 1 st at beg of next 4 rows (29 sts). Cont dec 1 st at neck edge, but at the same time bind off 13 sts at shoulder edge on next row and 14 sts on the next 2 alt rows.

Left front
Work as for right front, reversing shapings.

Sleeves
Using No. 7 needles and main color, cast on 36 sts. K1, p1 rib for 15 rows, inc 18 sts evenly along last row of rib (54 sts). Change to No. 10 needles and, beginning with a knit row, follow chart in st st, inc 1 st each end of 4th and every following 4th row until you have 84 sts. Work straight until chart is complete. Bind off loosely.

Finishing
Backstitch shoulder seams and, using flat seams, join sleeves to body, sew sleeve and side seams.

Neckband
With RS of work facing, using No. 7 needles and main color, pick up 17 sts up right front neck, 30 sts across back and 17 sts down left front neck (64 sts). K1, p1 rib for 9 rows. Bind off loosely in ribbing. Turn neckband inwards and sl st bound off edge to pick-up edge.

Buttonband
Using No. 7 needles and main color, cast on 8 sts. K1, p1 rib until band fits to *top* of neckband when slightly stretched. Bind off in ribbing.

Buttonhole band
Using No. 7 needles and main color, cast on 8 sts. K1, p1 for 4 rows. 5th row: rib 3, bind off 2, rib 3. On next row: rib 3, cast on 2, rib 3. Place 7 pins evenly up buttonband (placing last pin 3 rows before last bound off row). Make 7 more buttonholes as described, matching with pin positions. Bind off. Stitch bands into place.

SQUARE DANCE JUMPER

A dropped-sleeve, shawl-collared, mohair jumper in bright, bold colors. It is simple to knit, using stockinette stitch and the intarsia method, and snug to wear on cold, frosty days. The instructions are given in one size to fit chest sizes 34-37in.

Materials
Yarnworks mohair – 16oz of main color; 1¾oz each of four contrasting colors.
Needles
(Medium size) one pair of No. 7 and one pair of No. 9 needles.
Gauge
Using No. 9 needles and measured over st st, 16 sts and 20 rows = 4in square.

The chart overleaf (page 104) should be incorporated into the front of the sweater, the one on page 105 into the back.

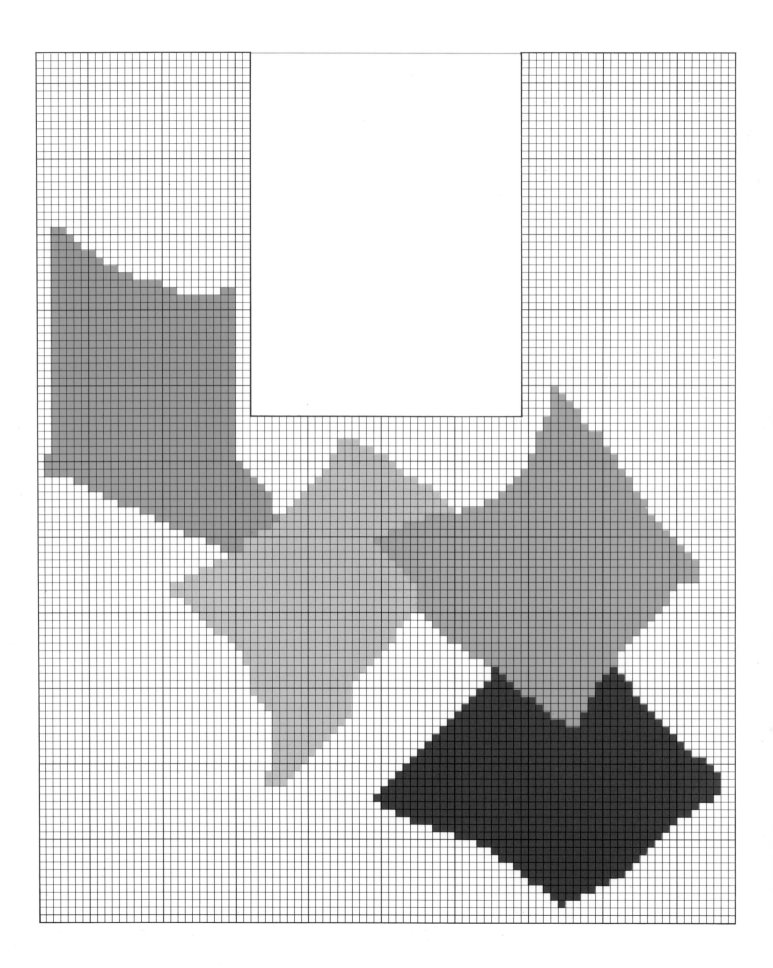

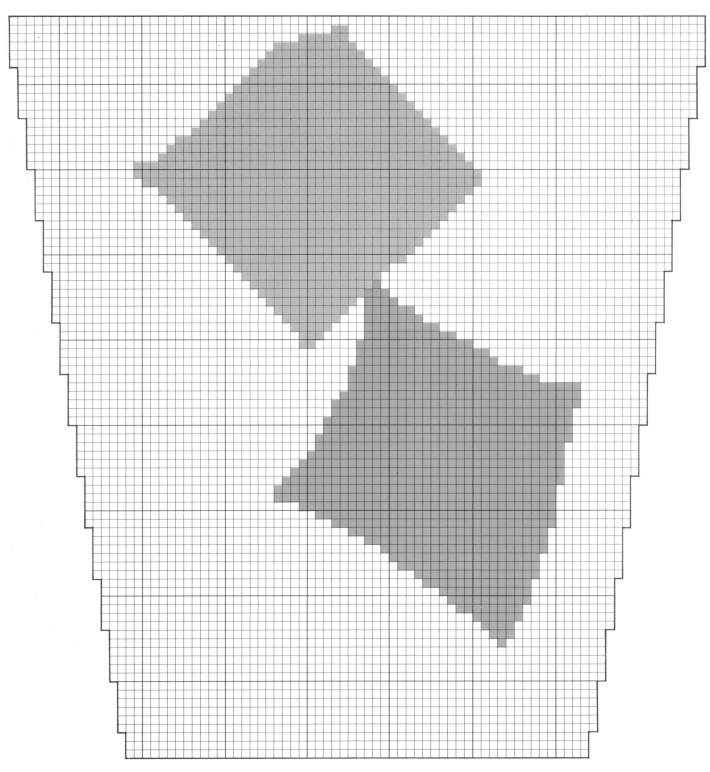

Incorporate the above chart into the left sleeve and the chart on page 107 into the right sleeve.

Back

Using No. 7 needles and main color, cast on 86 sts. K1, p1 rib for 3¼in, inc 9 sts evenly along last row of rib (95 sts). Change to No. 9 needles and cont in st st, following chart and beginning with a knit row. Work straight to row 115. Bind off 29 sts, place a marker, bind off 37 sts, place a marker, bind off remaining 29 sts.

Front

Work as for back to row 66, following the chart. Next row: still following the chart, work 29 sts, bind off center 37 sts, work to end. Working each side separately, cont following chart to row 115. Bind off.

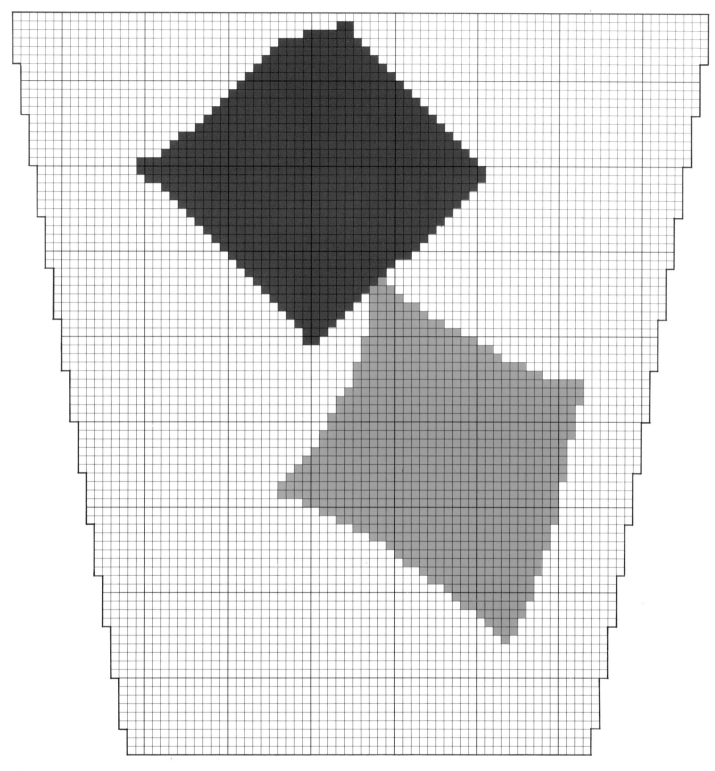

Sleeves

Using No. 7 needles and main color, cast on 38 sts. K1, p1 rib for 3¼in, inc 18 sts evenly along last row of rib (56 sts). Change to No. 9 needles and cont in st st, following the charts and inc 1 st each end of 3rd row and every following 6th row until you have 84 sts. Work 5 rows straight, bind off.

Collar

Using No. 7 needles and main color, cast on 142 sts. K1, p1 rib for 7½in. Change to color "C" and work in ribbing for 3 more rows. Bind off in ribbing using a No. 9 needle.

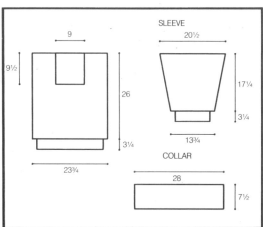

Finishing

Securely sew in all loose ends. Backstitch shoulder seams and, using a flat seam, join sleeve and side seams. When sewing sleeves to body, be careful to pull the underarm seams down to avoid puckering. Sew collar into position, crossing left front over right (*see* illustration, page 40).

SWAGGER JACKET AND COAT

Worked sideways from cuff edge to cuff edge, the main garment is worked in simple stockinette stitch. The full swagger effect is created by clever finishing. A one-size

garment, it will fit up to a size 14. The instructions are given for jacket/coat lengths throughout.

Materials
Yarnworks mohair – jacket: 28oz; coat: 35oz.
Needles
One pair of No. 6 and one pair of No. 8 needles.
Gauge
Using No. 8 needles and measured over st st, 18 sts and 24 rows = 4in square.

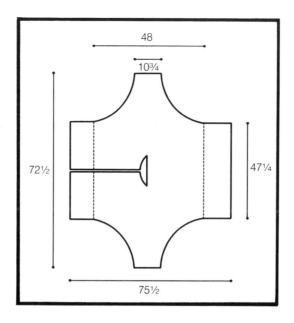

Measurements shown on diagram: 48, 10¾, 72½, 47¼, 75½

Pattern

Row 1 (RS): knit. Row 2: purl. Repeat these 2 rows 5 times more.
Row 13: purl. Row 14: knit. Repeat these 2 rows 6 times more.
These 26 rows form the pattern of alt bands of st st and rev st st. **NOTE:** Work in pattern throughout unless otherwise instructed.

JACKET AND COAT

(Worked in one piece from cuff to cuff.)
Using No. 9 needles, cast on 50 sts and work in pattern, inc 1 st each end of every 3rd row until you have 82 sts. Work 1 row straight. Now inc 1 st each end of next and every following alt row until you have 116 sts. Work 1 row straight. Now inc 1 st each end of every row until you have 138 sts. This point is the end of the sleeve.
Cast on 13/31 sts at beg of next 6 rows (216/324 sts). Now work straight until 7 patterns have been completed from cuff edge. Work 15 more rows in pattern, ending with an RS row.
Shape neck: work pattern over 108/162 sts, put these on to a thread to hold them and cont with remaining sts, binding off 2 sts and working to end. Work 1 row straight. Bind off 2 sts at beg of next and every following 6th row until 98/152 sts remain. Now work straight until 9 patterns have been worked from the cuff edge. Bind off evenly, keeping the gauge the same as the work itself as this will form the right front edge.
Return to the held sts, joining in the yarn at the neck edge, with RS facing. Cont working in pattern from where you left off, until 9 patterns have been worked from cuff edge. Work 22 more rows in pattern, then put aside.

Left front

Using No. 8 needles, carefully cast on 98/152 sts (this will form the left front edge). Work in pattern, starting on row 13. Work 15 rows straight.
Shape neck: cast on 2 sts at beg of next row, work to end. Cont casting on 2 sts at beg of every 6th row until you have 106/160 sts. Work 1 row straight. Cast on 2 sts at beg of next row and work to end. Now work across all front sts, then across the back sts which were put aside (216/324 sts). Work straight until 13 patterns have been worked from cuff edge. Work 16 more rows in pattern, ending with a WS row. Bind off 13/31 sts at beg of next 6 rows. Now dec 1 st each end of every row until 116 sts remain. Work 1 row straight, then dec 1 st each end of every alt row until 80 sts remain. Now dec 1 st each end of every 3rd row until 50 sts remain. Work 3 rows straight. Bind off.

Collar

Using No. 6 needles, cast on 29 sts. Work in k1, p1 rib, casting on 6 sts at beg of next 12 rows (101 sts). Work 6in straight from this point in the work, not the beg. Now bind off 6 sts at beg of next 12 rows, leaving 29 sts once again. Bind off loosely in ribbing.

Cuffs

Using No. 6 needles and with RS of work facing, knit up 34 sts evenly along the cuff edge. Work in k1, p1 rib for 2½in. Bind off loosely.

Finishing

Join the sleeve and side seams with a flat seam over the ribbing and a backstitch over the pattern. Lay the garment perfectly flat and mark the fold point along the shoulder and down the top of the sleeve with a row of safety-pins. Turn the garment inside out and run a thread of mohair along this line, skimming the "rough" bands of the pattern on the inside of the work so that it does not show through to the RS of work. By securing the thread at the beg of every "smooth" band and then jumping to the other side of it and pulling the thread tightly tog and securing again, the fabric becomes puckered with the rev st st ridges standing up on the RS of the work, while the st st bands lie flat (*see* illustration overleaf).
When the neck edge is reached, cont the thread around the back neck, but gathering rather than pulling the work up into ridges. Stitch down the second sleeve as for the first.

Fold the collar in two, right sides tog and close the rows' end edges with a flat seam. Turn it RS out, then pin the bound-off edge around the neck, RS to RS of main work, stopping ½in short of the front edges to allow these to curl. Work a narrow backstitch, then bring the cast-on edge of the collar over and slip st this down, just within the previous backstitch line on the inside of the neck.

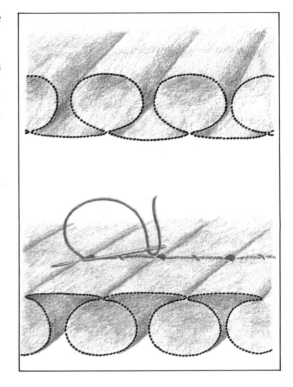

STOLE AND MUFF

A cunningly worked mock-ermine stole with muff.

Materials
Yarnworks mohair – stole:
20oz of natural, 1oz of black
mohair; muff: 7oz natural.
Needles
One pair of No. 8 needles.
Gauge
Using No. 8 needles and
measured over st st, 18 sts
and 24 rows = 4in square.

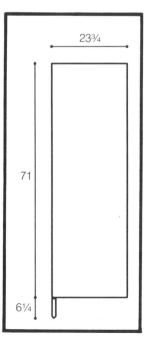

113

STOLE

Using No. 8 needles and natural, cast on 324 sts and work in pattern as follows:
Row 1 (WS): knit. Row 2: purl. Repeat last 2 rows 5 times more. Row 13: purl. Row 14: knit. Repeat last 2 rows 4 times more.
These 22 rows form the pattern. Work 8 patterns in all and then rows 1-12 inclusive. Bind off.

Tails
(Work 18 in all.)
Using No. 8 needles and natural, cast on 25 sts.
Row 1 (WS): k to last 2 sts, p1, change to black, p1. Row 2: black p1, M1, k1, change to natural, k1, p to end. Cont as set, inc the number of sts worked in black by 1 on every row until you have 31 sts. Now dec 1 st on every row at tail tip edge until you have 25 sts, all worked in natural. Bind off.

MUFF

Using No. 8 needles and natural, cast on 132 sts and work in pattern. Work 6 patterns in all, then rows 1-12 inclusive. Bind off.

Finishing
Stole: each pattern comprises 2 bands, then st st band and the rev st st band. Attach the tail along the end of row edges, one to every rev st st band, starting with that at the cast-on edge and finishing with the band worked before binding off. When the ends have been secured, brush the tips of the tail so that the outline becomes furry.
Muff: join the end of row edges with a flat seam to form a tube.

TIE-NECK JUMPER

Materials
Yarnworks mohair – 16oz.
Needles
One pair of No. 7 and one
pair of No. 8 needles.
Gauge
Using No. 8 needles and
measured over st st, 18 sts
and 24 rows = 4in square.

A stylish tie-neck jumper with dropped
sleeves, worked entirely in stockinette stitch.

Front
Using No. 7 needles, cast on 88 sts. K1, p1 rib
for 3¼in, inc 16 sts evenly across last row of rib
(104 sts). Change to No. 8 needles and,
beginning with a knit row, work straight in st
st until the front measures 17¾in from the beg
of your work, ending with an RS row.* **Shape
neck**: next row (WS): p 50 sts (leave these sts
on a spare needle, bind off center 4 sts, p 50
sts. Working each side of the neck separately,
dec 2 sts at neck edge every 3rd row until 27 sts
remain. Work straight until work measures
26¾in from the beg, bind off loosely. Repeat
for other side of neck.

Back
Work as for front to *. Bind off 27 sts loosely,
mark place with a colored thread, bind off 50
sts, mark with a thread, bind off remaining 27
sts.

Sleeves
Using No. 7 needles, cast on 38 sts and work in
k1, p1 rib for 3¼in, inc 18 sts evenly across last
row of rib (56 sts). Change to No. 8 needles
and, beginning with a knit row, work in st st,
inc 1 st each end of every 5th row until you
have 86 sts. Cont in st st without shaping until

work measures 16¼in. Bind off loosely.

Collar
Using No. 7 needles, cast on 240 sts. K1, p1 rib
for 6¾in. Bind off loosely in ribbing.

Toggle
Using No. 7 needles, cast on 10 sts. St st for
6in. Bind off.

Finishing
Join front back and sleeves with flat seams.
Backstitch shoulder seams matching the
markers and set in the sleeves, pulling them
down as you sew to avoid puckering. Join the
short ends of the toggle to make a ring, sew the
collar to the neck opening, leaving
approximately 8in at each end. Thread the
loose ends through the toggle and secure at
center neck opening.

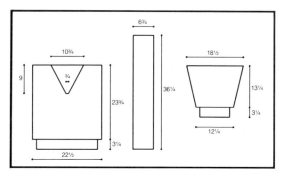

JAMBOREE CREW-NECK SWEATER

A multi-colored, patchwork, crew-neck sweater, using fairisle and intarsia methods worked in stockinette stitch.

Materials
Yarnworks mohair – 5oz black; 3½oz each of yellow and red; 1¾oz blue; 1oz each of orange, turquoise, fuchsia and white.
Needles
One pair of No. 7 and one pair of No. 10 needles.
Gauge
Using No. 10 needles and measured over st st, 16 sts and 18 rows = 4in square.

The chart opposite (page 119) should be incorporated into both the front and the back of the sweater. The top chart on page 120 should be incorporated into the left sleeve and the lower chart on page 120 into the right sleeve.

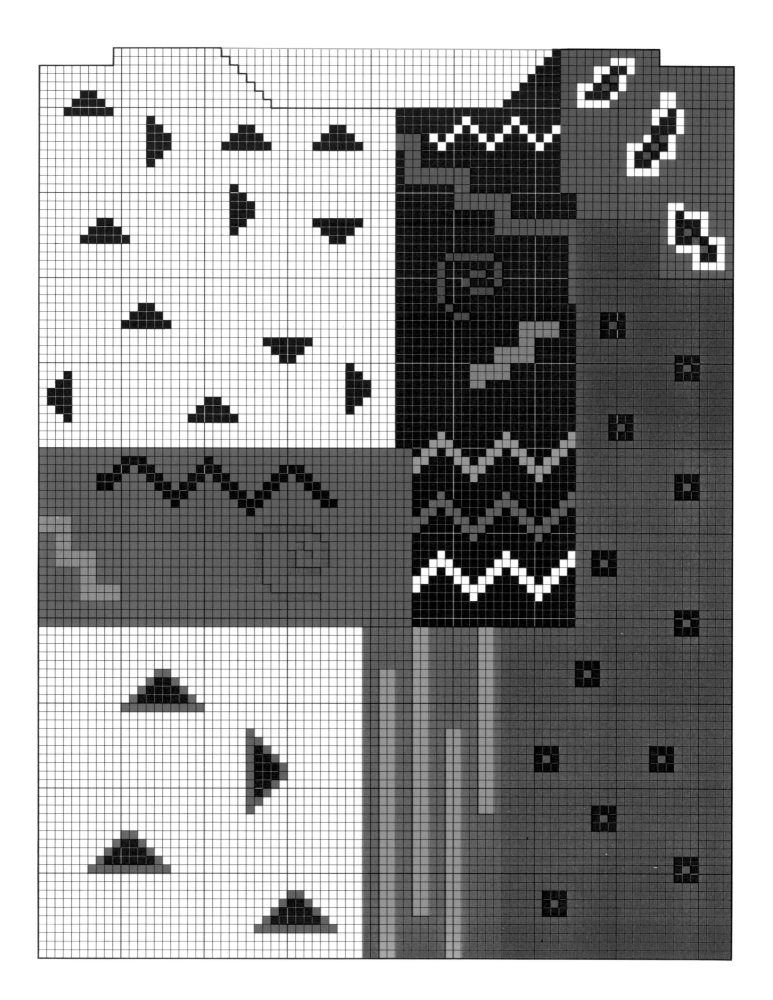

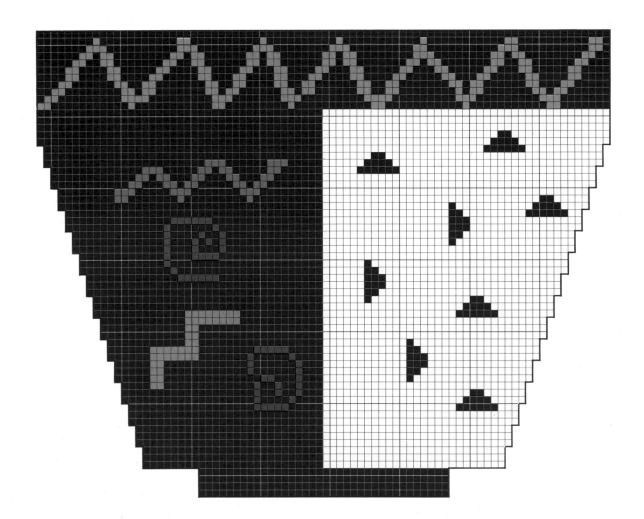

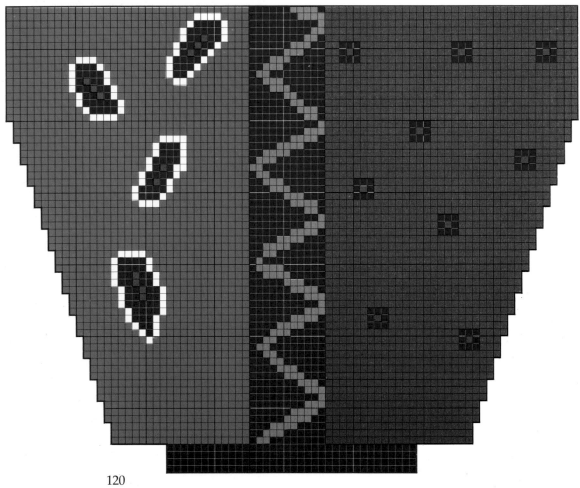

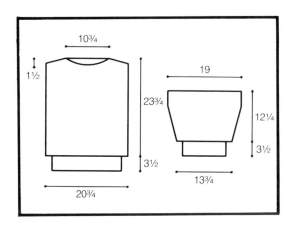

Front

Using No. 7 needles and black, cast on 70 sts. K1, p1 rib for ¾in, ending with a WS row. Next row: * rib 4, inc in next st. Repeat from * 13 times more (84 sts). Change to No. 10 needles and begin following the chart in st st, starting with a knit row. Work straight until 99 rows have been completed. **Shape neck**: row 100: p 28 sts (leave these sts on a spare needle). Bind off 28 sts, p 28 sts. Working on this last set of 28 sts, dec 1 st at neck edge on the next 6 rows. Next row: still dec 1 st at neck edge, bind off 9 sts at beg of row for the shoulder. Work 1 row, bind off remaining 13 sts. Rejoin yarn at neck edge of held sts. Repeat for other side of neck, reversing shapings.

Back

Work as for front, omitting the neck shaping.

Right sleeve

Using No. 7 needles and black, cast on 36 sts. K1, p1 rib for 3½in, inc 20 sts evenly in last row of rib (56 sts). Change to No. 10 needles and cont following sleeve chart in st st, inc 1 st each end of every 3rd row until you have 82 sts. Work straight without shaping for 25 more rows. Bind off loosely.

Left sleeve

Work as for right sleeve but following left sleeve chart. Backstitch left shoulder seams together.

Neckband

With RS of work facing, No. 7 needles and black, pick up 7 sts down right front side; 28 sts center front; 7 sts up left front side; and 40 sts from center back (82 sts). K1, p1 rib for 9 rows. Bind off loosely in ribbing. Turn neckband inwards and stitch bound-off edge to "pick-up" edge.

Finishing

Backstitch remaining shoulder seam, using flat seams. Join sleeves to body; join side and sleeve seams.

SMOKING JACKET

A traditional smoking-jacket look for women. A one-size jacket, worked mainly in stockinette stitch, with raglan sleeves. The shawl collar and turn-back cuffs are worked in moss stitch and the fastenings are braided frogs.

Back

Using No. 7 needles, cast on 104 sts. Next row: * p1, k1, rep from * to end. Row 2: * k1, p1, rep from * to end. Keep repeating these 2 rows to form moss st. Work 6 rows in all, then change to No. 8 needles and cont in st st until work measures 14¼in, ending with a WS row.

Shape raglan: bind off 2 sts at beg of next 2 rows. Next row: k2, sl1, k1, psso, k to last 4 sts, k2 tog, k2. Row 2: purl. Keep repeating these 2 rows until 32 sts remain.
** Next row (WS): p2, p2 tog, p to last 3 sts, sl last st worked from RH needle to LH needle, lift the next st on the LH needle over it and return it to the RH needle, p2. Row 2: k2, sl1, k1, psso, k to last 4 sts, k2 tog, k2.** Repeat these 2 rows until 20 sts remain. Bind off.

Right front

Using No. 7 needles, cast on 58 sts and work 6 rows in moss st. Change to No. 8 needles. Next row (RS): moss st 4, k to end. Row 2: p to last 4 sts, moss st 4. Keep repeating these 2 rows until the work measures 9¾in, ending with a WS row.
Next row: bind off 4 sts, k to end. Cont in st st until work measures 14¼in, ending with an RS row.
Shape raglan: bind off 2 sts, p to end. Next row: k to last 4 sts, k2 tog, k2. Row 2: purl. Repeat these last 2 rows once more.
Shape neck: meanwhile cont to shape raglan, as set, dec 1 st at neck edge on next and every following 5th row until 11 decs have been made at this edge in all. Now work this edge straight but cont with raglan, shaping until 7 sts remain.
Next row (WS): p2, p2 tog, p to end. Row 2: k2, k2 tog, k2. Row 3: p1, p2 tog, p2. Row 4: k1, k2 tog, k1. Row 5: p2 tog, p1. K the last 2 sts tog. Fasten off.

Left front

Work as for the right front, reversing shapings.

Sleeves

Using No. 7 needles, cast on 80 sts and work in moss st until the sleeve measures 4¾in. Change to No. 8 needles and cont in st st, inc 1 st each end of every 5th row until you have 104 sts. Work straight until sleeve measures 14½in from beg, ending with a WS row.
Shape raglan: as for back until 46 sts remain. Now work from ** to ** until 6 sts remain. Bind off.

Collar

Using No. 7 needles, cast on 4 sts and work in moss st, inc 1 st at end of 1st row. Cont to inc 1 st at this edge on every row until you have 12 sts. Now inc 1 st at this edge on every alt row until you have 22 sts. Work straight for 30in, measured from the last shaping row. Now dec to shape the second half to match the first. Bind off the 4 sts remaining.

Finishing

Join the raglans, side and sleeve seams, using a flat seam. Divide the collar and neck into sections so as to distribute the collar evenly

Materials
Yarnworks mohair – 23oz. 1 pair of raglan shoulder pads; 2 pairs of black braided frog fastenings.
Needles
One pair of No. 7 and one pair of No. 8 needles.
Gauge
Using No. 8 needles and measured over st st, 18 sts and 24 rows = 4in square.

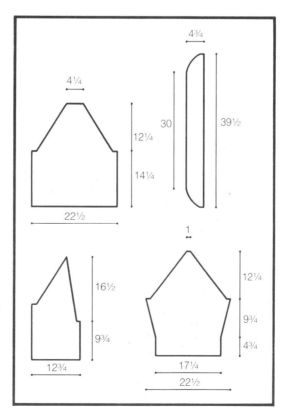

between the 2 points on the fronts where the 4 border sts were bound off (the cast-on and bound-off edges of the collar are attached to these edges). Pin and sew with a flat seam, the shaped edge of the collar being the outer edge, which is not attached. Pin the fastenings into position, as in the photograph. Attach from the WS of work, using ordinary sewing thread of an appropriate color.

CARING FOR YOUR MOHAIR GARMENTS

As with all knitwear, mohair garments should not be hung or they will drop and become mis-shapen on the shoulders. Instead, they should be stored flat and carefully folded to minimize creasing.

Dry cleaning is recommended for all mohair since it enhances the fluffiness of the fiber and maintains far more elasticity in a garment than constant washing will do. Pressing is not necessary and should be avoided.

Washing will tend to flatten and slightly matt the fibers, but if this method is preferable use a mild detergent or soap. Squeeze the water out of the garment rather than holding it up and letting the weight of the water pull the garment out of shape. Rinse thoroughly, adding a fabric conditioner. Dry flat, pressing the garment into its correct shape. When the garment is completely dry, it may have the fluffiness restored by a gentle brushing, using light strokes so that the bristles do not pull individual stitiches or by a very brief period in a tumble dryer – three rotations maximum.

NOTE: A mohair garment should only ever be put into a dryer when it has already been completely dried and then only for the briefest of tumbles.

YARN INFORMATION

All the sample garments illustrated in this book were knitted in Yarnworks Luxury Kid mohair. As many of the designs contain small quantities of several different colors, Yarnworks offers individual kits containing only the quantities of yarn necessary to complete each garment. In addition, buttons, embroidery threads and trimmings are included where appropriate.

To order, simply contact Marcus Corps, 117 Dobbins Street, Brooklyn, New York 11222.

For those who wish to substitute different yarns, weights are given throughout to the nearest 1oz ball whenever necessary. Each 1oz ball of Yarnworks mohair is approximately 53 yards. To obtain the best results you must ensure that the gauge recommended on your selected yarn *matches the gauge* printed in our pattern. We cannot guarantee your results if this rule is not followed.